Cats

in the

Parsonage II

CLAIR SHAFFER, JR.

Evergreen
PRESS

Cats in the Parsonage II
by Clair Shaffer, Jr.
Copyright ©2004 Clair Shaffer, Jr.

ISBN 1-58169-157-2
For Worldwide Distribution
Printed in the U.S.A.

Evergreen Press
P.O. Box 191540 • Mobile, AL 36619

Table of Contents

Dedication

To my beautiful wife, Brenda,
who, despite all my faults and flaws,
still loves me and puts up with me.
She is truly a blessed "help-mate"
in every sense of the word.
May God bless her ever so richly.

INTRODUCTION

I have been pleased with the reception of the first *Cats in the Parsonage* across the country. I am thrilled that cat lovers have responded so well to the story of Taffy and Tiffany, our little prized pussycats. It was a pleasure for me to write it and share the love and the bond my wife, Brenda, and I formed with Taff and Tiff. I hope that our story has encouraged and inspired readers to truly esteem their pets and to see the hand of God in bringing humans and animals together. I also hope and pray that it stirred the minds and hearts of many people to consider giving the Lord Jesus a place in their lives. He is the One who can bring us all together in true harmony, love, and peace.

In the wake of September 11, 2001, we saw a resurgence of faith and patriotism in our nation and many astute Americans do not want to see it go by the wayside. The ever-present threat of terrorism has made us appreciate more what we have in this country and we need to live better, grateful lives. "911" brings a deeper implication than just a date or an emergency number. Christians are aware of a more important 911 and that is Psalm 91:1.

The one who lives in the shelter of the Most High, will rest in the shadow of the Almighty.

When we have a proper relationship with God through His Son, Jesus Christ, it does not matter what tragedy or trial may invade our lives, we will not be shattered and driven to despair. We will "rest secure" in the shadow of our God. In Him we find real happiness, meaning, and purpose—the incentive to do our best.

So now, here's *Cats in the Parsonage II*. The adventures of Taffy and Tiffany did not end when I completed their first book. The little scamps went on to wow and amaze us with some more cute escapades and heart-touching acts of love and feline insight. So sit back, kick up, and please enjoy the sequel, and may God bless you!

—*Clair F. Shaffer, Jr.*

"Ask the animals
and they will teach you."

Job 12:7

CHAPTER 1

I NEVER MET A CAT I DIDN'T LIKE
(ALMOST)

W ill Rogers made the above statement about men, but I have often wondered if he ever met some exasperating characters who caused him a bit of consternation. I find myself reacting to animals much in the same way I react to people. With my lower nature still firmly intact, too often I am tempted to make snap judgments without giving the person or animal a chance to let me get to know them better. It's called not practicing what you preach. This was the case with a cat that came into our area a few years ago.

"FROG AND SCRUFFY"

Some years ago a little light gray and white kitty showed up in our neighborhood and the kids named her Frog. Just where she came from is not certain, but she is certainly a cat with a lot of mettle. She reminds me of Candy, the original "Parsonage Cat" and grandmother of Taffy and Tiffany. Frog doesn't take anything from anybody including people. I started to roughhouse with her one day out back, and apparently she thought I was trying to hurt her. Little vixen! She came at me with tooth and claw, and I barely escaped unscathed.

On the other hand, she is very loving and a caring mother with her kittens. Frog nurses them far beyond the normal time and allows them and other cats to eat first at the feeding dishes. She enjoys being petted and being with people. She is just a nice cat!

One day when Brenda went out back, Frog came running across the lawn from next door. As Brenda knelt down to pet Frog, she noticed a large nasty gash on top of her head. It was laying open and was dirty and very close to being infected. My compassionate partner quickly applied some antibacterial ointment to Frog's injury and gave her something to eat. She had some other minor cuts and scratches that clearly showed that the kitty had been in quite a scrap.

The wound healed nicely since Brenda continued to put more ointment on the cut, but not too long after the first incident, it happened again. This time it was worse. Dr. Brenda went to work once more, and Frog seemed to enjoy the attention and treatment. However, we were concerned about how and why this was happening. Up to this point, no one had seen Frog fighting with another cat or animal.

Then one of our neighbors saw a huge black and white, longhaired tom-cat stalking Frog and trying to mate with her. Brenda saw him and called me to take care of the bully who was inflicting the terrible injuries on our little friend. Whenever any of us caught sight of him around our homes, we chased him; but this guy was persistent and was not easily discouraged.

He was a mangy looking sight, his white fur appearing sort of yellowish, and the rest of him in dire need of grooming. He was big—my guess was about 25 pounds, and the other cats—both toms and females—were scared of him. Louise grabbed a rake or whatever she could when he came around. As small as our neighbor is, we were afraid that this tom might try to drag her off, so we warned Louise not to turn her back on him.

Because of his disheveled appearance, I nicknamed him "Scruffy" and the title stuck. He may have been called other names, but I do not wish to dwell on them. In any event, everyone agreed that my designation for this "nasty boy" was quite appropriate. Our ordeal with Scruffy went on for some time because he refused to leave our neighborhood, and all efforts to persuade him that he was not welcome completely failed. He also rejected our attempts to win him over and continued to terrorize the outdoor cats.

Finally, we heard a rumor that someone separated his nine lives from him all at one time. I feel compelled to say that it was not Bill, our neighbor, who felt that he was portrayed similar to an "executioner" in Cats I. That certainly was not my intention as Bill is a farmer who cares for his animals very well and has been seen carrying a cat or two around in an affectionate manner. Please don't repeat that—I wouldn't want it to get back to Marty Raker, one of my parishioners and a good friend of Bill's, who may think he's gettin' soft. (Bill and Marty are farmer/construction/mechanic/machinist workers who really know what it is to put in a full day of hard labor. They have been friends for a long time and are there to help when someone is in need. I can testify to that personally.)

I must say that I felt no compunction over Scruffy's demise. In fact, I think that everyone in our neighborhood was relieved that he was gone and no longer harming their cats. Little Frog, I'm sure was happy not to be harassed and hurt by this huge bully. This was one of the few cats I ever met that I didn't like.

"PEACHY"

She was another of the neighborhood strays or barn cats we have been privileged to know. Peachy was a gold angora with beautiful silky hair, probably so named because of her color. She had an attractive personality and disposition, always friendly and pleasant—one of those "special" felines. It was a pleasure to pet and hold this little gal who just made you feel good to be around her. All of us loved little Peachy, and I heard a rumor that like a couple of the other favorites, she was invited into homes pretty close to us. As I recall, she was in our back room a few times for a treat away from the cats on the back porch. It was hard to resist her charm.

Like other female cats in our corner of the world, Peachy got in a family way. I suppose that we all watched and cared for her a little more than we did the rest of the pregnant pussycats. We couldn't help ourselves! She just won us over.

Like most cats with kittens, Peachy tended to be somewhat protective, especially if strangers came around. She didn't mind us making a fuss over her babies too much, but still there was a limit to her patience. One day, after a lot of coddling and handling by too many people, Peachy took drastic action.

Barb was outside next door and noticed the little mommy carrying her young ones, one by one, to a safer place. As Barb carefully followed Peachy, staying just far enough behind, she saw where this ingenious kitty was hiding her brood. She was amazed and tickled at the same time.

Years ago, after Brenda and I had moved into the parsonage and the garage was repaired, I built a cupola with a weathervane and put it on the roof. Now it was sturdy and painted, but it was made of wood and the rain and snow and sun had taken their toll. I'm also sure that many falling walnuts from the big tree above it had a diverse effect upon it. As a result, the cupola had a hole in one side of the roof and guess who found it?

Yup! If you guessed "Peachy," you guessed right. Somehow that tiny tot located this spot high up where most humans would fear to tread and deposited her kitties inside. Now the hole in the roof wasn't that big, but Peachy squeezed in and neatly laid her babies on the side away from the opening to keep them out of the rain. The weather at this time was mild so there was no problem with snow or ice. I did not put a floor in the cupola so the kitties were laying on the slanted roof of the garage. No problem! Peachy arranged them in such a fashion that none of them were on top of another and in danger of smothering.

How did she get up on the garage roof, you might ask? That was no problem for our clever kitty. I had built a small shed on the field side of the garage made of wafer board and a shingle roof. The garage roof was a heavy gauge metal but was not slippery. Peach, with sharp claws, went right up the side of the shed onto its roof and then up the garage room to the cupola. She made at least four or five trips like this until she had every one of her kitties all snuggled together.

I am not sure just how long she left them in the cupola, but after a while she decided to move them again, this time to Louise's back porch. I helped Peachy move them and she did not seem to mind my assistance. This little beauty was just a pleasure to be around. I then dismantled the dilapidated cupola and disposed of it in the burn barrel.

After Peachy's kittens were old enough to be weaned, they were given new homes. And although we were glad to have Peachy around, we were all concerned about her safety. We remembered Sammy and Stinky and a few other cats we grew fond of, and we wanted a better fate for her. It was just too hazardous for an outdoor cat in our neighborhood. After doing some checking around, Barb found a nice family for our beloved Peachy, and we were all relieved and happy for her.

"PESTY"

If you have ever been around kittens, you know that they have boundless energy. There seems to be no end to their playful activities. Some tend to have more vitality than others. This was the case with Warren and Nancy Shipe's Kitty whom they fitly named "Pesty." Bud and Nancy are members of our St. Elias Church and some time ago we were at their home for a visit where we had the distinct pleasure of meeting the new feline addition to their family.

When we first moved here, Bud and Nancy had a black long-haired cat named Blackie. Now, after reaching a good old age, their friend was gone, and they were feeling the pain of the separation. Family and friends suggested getting another cat right away to fill the void. Cats, and other pets, are good therapy for us humans and I'm sure that is one reason God put them here.

Well, when we arrived at Bud and Nancy's, we were greeted by a little gold and white whirlwind who was running to and fro, leaping and jumping as if he was on speed. I think my first question to our hosts was something like, "Who wound him up?" Nancy cautioned us to keep an eye on him at all times because he would strike out at anything that moved. Of course, anything that moves is fair game to any cat, or so a cat thinks! Pesty was convinced of this feline belief, and he was fully armed, i.e., he still had all his claws.

After seating ourselves on the sofa, little Pesty had to give us the once over, and being cat lovers, we wanted to hold and pet him. This was nigh unto impossible because the tiny fireball wouldn't stay still long enough for any offer of affection. If you tried to hold him, you did it at your own risk! When he wanted to leave, he was one determined little pussycat.

We noticed right away that the main target of Pesty's playful machinations was Bud, who stands well over six feet, and when sitting down cannot hide too well. Now, Nancy did not say that her husband "teased" the kitty. I believe the word she used was "encouraged." If Bud made one move, especially with his hand, Pesty was on him, biting and digging in with those very sharp talons. Brenda and I admired Bud's patience and endurance with the little guy who was an endless flurry of activity.

The main thing I remember about our visit that evening was when Nancy went to get some refreshments and Brenda accompanied her to help. I noticed that Pesty followed them into the kitchen apparently hoping for a handout or just curious to see what they were up to. Now the girls were not gone that long, but before they had a chance to return with the goodies, Pesty made a grand return entrance.

Bud and I were talking and were sort of oblivious to the quiet and calm that had pervaded the living room in Pesty's absence. All of a sudden, without warning, the kitty was back! He came running into the room at breakneck speed and leaped into the air, landing on Bud's lap with teeth and feet going in uninterrupted action. I swear that the cat was airborne for eight to ten feet! All I saw was a gold and white blur until he landed on Bud, surprising my friend and causing him to extract the kitty from his legs with a few "ow's" and "ouches."

Once Bud had separated the little demon from his claw-hold, he held him up in the air and said to him, "Look, you little brat!" Mild words compared to what some people would have used. About this time, Nancy and Brenda came in with the refreshments and Nancy said, "You can easily see why we named him Pesty." This little guy wanted to be where the action was, and if there was not enough action to suit him, he created his own.

We enjoyed the rest of our visit with Bud and Nancy, of course, and were entertained by Pesty right up to the time we left. He was certainly full of life and making the most of it as we all should do. Today, a few years later, Pesty is a grown cat and has slowed down a bit, but he still likes to play and be in the center of things. He has brought a lot of joy and companionship to Bud and Nancy, and we are sure that is why he was sent into their lives.

"D. C."

Not too many years after Brenda and I became Pastor and wife at Zion and St. Elias, one of our families' homes was destroyed by fire. All of a sudden, Pete and Clara Boone and their son, Peter, lost everything they had worked for. I remember getting the call from another of our ladies, Connie Yagel, who lived nearby. Brenda and I were on our way to make a visit, so she dropped me off at Barbara Sassaman's house. Barbara (Pete and Clara's daughter) and her husband Charles—whom we call "Sass"—lived near her parents' home and had a full view of the fire. Brenda then went on to see the people we had intended to visit and then returned to Barbara's. Clara and Pete were there with Barbara for safety and support, and after a feeble attempt to comfort them, I walked up to the fire scene while Brenda stayed with Clara.

I saw Pete standing by one of the firemen and so I came up to him and put my hand on his shoulder. We said nothing. We looked at each other, hugged, and cried. A fire is a terrible thing. In a short period of time your prized possessions representing treasured memories become only memories! It is a devastating experience.

Pete and Clara needed a place to stay until they could rebuild. After a few days with Barbara and Sass, they were offered an apartment with Bob and Connie Yagel just at the end of their road. There were three very nice apartments in the large house remodeled by another of our members, Ray Radel. The lower level one was vacant, and Pete and Clara accepted.

We knew that Bob and Connie wanted to sell their home, and the situation seemed right for Pete and Clara. With Pete's health declining, he felt it would be better to buy a home rather than go through the hassle of rebuilding. So they struck a deal and Bob and Connie built a new home closer to Line Mountain High School where their son, Kris, was involved in sports and academic activities. Kris eventually became the first Line Mountain graduate to attend and graduate from West Point. He personally recruited a friend a year behind him who became the second West Point graduate from the high school.

All of this is by way of introduction to tell of Bob and Connie's cat, "D.C."—"Dumb Cat." As it turned out, the gray tiger kitty was anything but dumb. Of course, when they moved to their new place near the high school, they took D.C. with them. Bob related to me how during the trip, the kitty observed all the details of the territory he was being transported through. Perhaps this "dumb cat" was making notes for future reference.

After being in their new residence a few days, Bob and Connie noticed that D.C. was nowhere to be found. They thought maybe he was just exploring his new turf. Not so! A few days later, Pete called to tell them that their pussycat was sunning himself on his porch! Mr. D.C. had gone home to more familiar surroundings.

The trek from his new home back to his old home is not terribly far for D.C., but it included a hike over the Dornsife Mountain. Imagine the dangers the little traveler could have encountered along the way. Despite all of that, D.C. was determined to get home, and he did! Bob and Connie may have wished that they had left him there because some time later he was shot and killed near their home. It's sad that some individuals get pleasure from harming these wonderful creatures of God. They truly need our prayers in more ways than one.

"ROCKY"

Whenever Brenda and I travel to see my sister and her husband about sixty some miles away, we get to see their cat, Rocky. This beautiful dark gray and white kitty has been with them for many years and is just a most pleasant chap to be around. He is an indoor/outdoor feline who likes his freedom to roam over their 52-acre farm. Rocky would not be happy being a completely indoor cat, although if the door is open and an invitation is made, he will come in for a spell. He is affectionate but doesn't care to be held and fussed over for too long a time.

Like many cats, Rocky is an avid and able hunter who enjoys bringing his prize prey to show off to Nancy and Elwood. If they are not present when he returns from the hunt, he leaves the booty in a conspicuous place. They have found the usual variety of chipmunks, moles, and birds on the porch and other high-traffic areas as evidence of his prowess and, no doubt, as proof that he is fulfilling his part in contributing to the household provisions.

This, I think, is important to the pride of a cat who feels that he is a vital cog in the family machinery. Often, as many cat lovers can attest, cats regard themselves as the key "person" of the family. To the cat, he is the nucleus of the home, the glue that holds everything together, the indispensable member on this train of life. Rocky fits this to a tee, even though he is somewhat of a loner and cherishes his kitty cat independence. He shows up after being absent for a while with an air of "Okay, I'm here! Everything's going to be all right. Don't worry, just enjoy my company."

I enjoy Rocky's routine when our family gets together at Nancy and Elwood's annual July 4th picnic. Each year we are treated to barbecue chicken with Elwood's own special recipe, and more delicious food than anyone could ever hope to eat in a week. We all chip in and bring side dishes to compliment the yummy chicken, and I am always impressed with the creativity that the girls put into preparing these extras. For example my cousin, Shirley, came one year with a decorative ceramic boat, beautifully arranged with dip and veggies. She called it her "Dip Ship." No jokes, please!

Anyway, Rocky seems to love these get-togethers because everyone makes a fuss over him, and he gets some handouts from most of us. He nonchalantly meanders through the group, cooly accepting or rejecting the morsels offered to him. Once satisfied that he has had a taste of the best cuisine available, he either retires to a nearby spot on the perimeter of the gathering to observe us entrancing humans, or takes his leave to nap or peruse the countryside.

Now Rocky does well with Nancy and Elwood's other two pets—Tazzie, a pewter gray female cat, and Cooper, the newest addition to the Brininger family, a male Airedale. Although these two arrived on the scene a good time later than he did, Rocky accepts them but still lets them know that he is in charge of the establishment. In Rocky's mind, "He's da' man!"

Tazzie is a beauty and is one of those kitties you just want to pick up and love. She gets along well with Rocky and Cooper and would like to be inside on a full time basis. Cooper is a story in himself. He is very intelligent and continues to amaze Nancy and Elwood with things "a dog just shouldn't know how to do." He has been to obedience school and has a remarkable capacity to understand commands and signals. He's Elwood's "Buddy."

This is Rocky's world! He is content with it and in many ways shapes it to suit himself, maintaining that feline independence. Rock is in control and he likes it that way. I don't think he allows too much to bother him, and we can all learn from that—Christians especially. It's called resting in the Lord and letting things in His hand. There is always something we can glean from our animal friends.

"TOMMY"

It hurts to say good-bye to our pets when age or disease or some other cruel thing takes them from us. For Sally and John Aumiller, this was true when they had to have their cat, Buffy, put to sleep. A gold tiger, domestic short-hair, Buffy had been with them a long time and it was hard to let go. I remember the day Sally called me to share the news, and I could sympathize with their pain. I knew some day Brenda and I would be facing the same thing with Taff and Tiff. I tried, I'm sure in a feeble way, to offer some words of comfort to Sally and said a few prayers over the next several days to help her and John through their grief. I knew that God would somehow provide for them in His mysterious, loving way.

It wasn't too long before a little black and white kitty began spending time around their home and trying to woo their affections. He was successful in his attempts, but Sally and John found out that he belonged to their neighbor. They were disappointed until the people told them that they were welcome to the kitty and "Tommy" had a new home. Once again, prayers were answered, and God brought another one of His wonderful creatures into the lives of His children.

It wasn't a new experience for John and Sally adjusting to a kitten again after being "owned" by a mature cat, but it brought the usual excitement and precautions of having a young, untrained feisty feline loose in the house. All cat lovers know how much fun and enjoyment kittens can be, but they are also aware of the anxious moments these little critters can cause. Nice, soft, plush furniture must be watched and inspected; curtains and/or drapes and sheers need to be protected; glass, porcelain, and ceramic knick-knacks require positions of safety; beautifully finished wood items must be covered or moved to secure places. There is much more we could say in this area, but I think you get the picture, and we haven't even discussed the hazards to human body parts and clothing.

One of the secrets of raising a kitten is to spend as much time as possible with the little furball. This helps in establishing a good relationship with the kitty, it helps your pet feel secure and loved, and it lets him know what is permissible and what is not. That may sound strange when discussing the behavior of a cat, but it really is not because a cat can be trained just like a dog or any other pet, perhaps with a bit more effort and patience. With love, persistence, understanding, and a pinch of know-how, you can help to mold your kitten's personality so that you have a nice, very desirable companion. (It works on people, too.)

Now John loves football—high school to pro—and is an avid Penn State Nittany Lion fan. Sally is not a sports fan, but she tolerates her husband's emphatic interest in the subject and tries to console him when his team loses. He really used to feel down when the Lions didn't win, but eventually began to see setbacks as a part of life and applied this positive attitude to the realm of sports.

Like most serious sports fans in our area, John has paraphernalia from Penn State. One of these items is a blue and white pin-on button picturing the Nittany Lion and it plays the school fight song. Once, when John activated the button, Tommy was intrigued by the music and wanted to see this amazing piece of human ingenuity that produced such a cute noise. After John put it on the floor, Tommy promptly took his foot and turned it over, examined it closely, flipped it a few more times, and then picked it up using his teeth on the safety clasp pin on the back. He ran around the house with it and when it stopped playing, he brought it back to John to get it going again. Once in a while, he would step on it, and the music would play, much to his delight.

One evening Brenda and I were visiting with John and Sally, and John wanted to show us their Kitty's new obsession. As we watched from the living room, John went into the dining room and opened the bottom drawer of a bureau, reached in, and activated the Penn State button. Tommy, who had been playing on the floor with Brenda and I, rushed into the dining room, jumped into the drawer, and emerged with the button. He promptly brought it to us and dropped it on the floor, seemingly so proud of himself.

After it stopped playing, he batted it around a few times and then looked at us as if to say, "Okay, guys! What are you waiting for?" Brenda pushed the button, the music began, and Tommy was off toting the PSU button throughout the house. I said to John, "You ought to write to Coach Paterno and tell him he even has four-legged fans." We all laughed and enjoyed Tommy as he entertained us the rest of the evening.

We learned that Tommy has another favorite past time when Sally brushes his teeth at the bathroom sink. If this activity sounds a bit eccentric, it shouldn't because cats have plaque build up on their teeth and can develop gum disease like humans. Taff and Tiff have had their teeth cleaned and have been on antibiotics for gum infections. (This is something cat owners should periodically inspect in caring for their felines.)

Sally runs water in the sink to use to rinse Tommy's teeth and gums after cleaning his pearly whites. Now most cats do not like water other than to drink and detest bathing or any such ritual their humans subject them to. However, there are exceptions and Tommy is one of them. While Sally is attempting to give him some good dental hygiene, Tommy splashes a little mess for Sally, but she is happy that her Kitty cooperates in such an important procedure.

"SCOOTER"

Sally's parents, Dick and Floretta Meiser, also members of our Zion Church, were being solicited by a little black female feline. Probably the victim of a "drop off," the kitten did her best to win the affections of this nice, animal loving couple. Richard, as Floretta calls Dick when she means business, was not so easy to win over as his wife. He was more a dog person and not quite ready to accept this tiny black ball of fluff.

It certainly was not because the kitty didn't try. She ran to meet them every time they were outside, especially on the front porch. At first, she was a little shy and stayed at a distance, meowing and running around on the porch or wherever they happened to be. As time went on, she became a little braver, allowing them to pet her and wanting to get on their laps or lay beside them. All the time this was going on, Sally and John were encouraging them to adopt her as a pet. Dick and Floretta resisted somewhat, being reluctant to take on the responsibility of a small kitten. However, the kitty did not give up and continued to flatter them with her charm.

Finally, all the "smooze" the little tyke was spreading over them started to pay off. She began to be invited in the house on a trial basis. Well! Miss Pussycat knew that she liked this arrangement and did her best to show Dick and Floretta that she could be the perfect guest. Before too long, she had a home and a relationship began to grow and flourish between pet and people. When I asked them the name of the new addition to their family, Floretta told me the kitty's name was "Scooter," because she "scooted" here and there like a flash.

Sally and John were right—Scooter was good therapy for her Mom and Dad. The care and responsibility for their pet helped to focus their attention somewhat on something other than their health problems, especially Dick's serious kidney and heart conditions. I am convinced that Scooter's entrance into their lives at that time was no coincidence. I truly believe that she was heaven sent. Although Dick never completely accepted this cat, I saw him chuckle at the little squirt as she tried to fulfill her mission in bringing some joy into an otherwise bleak situation. She provided hours of entertainment and excitement and helped to get Dick's mind off his physically hopeless situation.

As his health further deteriorated, it was necessary to call in Hospice and the nurses did a fine, compassionate job. The next April, the Lord called Richard home to glory, and his pain and suffering evolved into perfect joy and wonder. A World War II veteran, Dick was a man's man who loved his country, worked hard all his life and believed in the Judeo-Christian principles and values this nation was founded on. He was a family man who loved and supported his children in all they did. He will be missed!

With Dick gone and her own health less than perfect, Floretta had some decisions to make, one of which was whether or not to stay by herself in their home of over 50 years. I'm sure that this was Floretta's first choice, and her son, David, and his wife, Joyce, and Sally lived only a short distance away. However, the maintenance of the house required going up and down steps and some other arduous tasks, so after this choice was considered, it was reluctantly eliminated.

It is still amazing to me how our loving Lord works things out for His children whom He loves more than they will ever know. The factory where Sally had worked for over 20 years closed down, and all of a sudden she was unemployed. It was also at this time that her parents' health began to be in jeopardy and Sally was available to help. We all agreed that God knew what was going to happen with Dick and Floretta's health and the plant shut-down. Sally took it as an indication from the Lord that her job now was to care for her parents.

After Dick was called home, Floretta moved in with Sally and John and sold her house to her grandson, Shaun and his wife, Heather. The homestead would be kept in the family. And what about Scooter? Well, what do you think? Yep! She went too and was accepted by Tommy who was elated to have a "buddy" on his own level. Scooter couldn't have hoped for anything better—three people who adore her and a fellow feline who welcomed her with open paws. If Scooter could speak our language, perhaps she would say, "It doesn't get any better than this!"

"PUDGE"

Ryan and Kelly Heim, one of our younger couples at St. Elias, have a kitty named "Pudge." We first met Pudge after Ryan and Kelly were married and moved into their new home in Sunbury. Ryan had her as a pet for a few years before he and Kelly tied the knot, so now she is a senior citizen. Kelly was used to cats and dogs while growing up so it was no problem for her when Ryan wanted to bring his buddy along to share their lives.

Pudge is a dark gray tiger with beautiful markings and a pleasant personality. On our first visit with Kelly and Ryan, of course I just had to pick the kitty up and snuggle her and talk baby-talk to her. She seemed to eat it up and tolerated my "can't-resist-loving-up-kitty-cats" obsession. I know that my wife and Kelly and

Ryan got a kick out of this scene in which a bystander may have thought I was holding a little baby. This is nothing unusual for me as I consider my furry friends as "babies" to cuddle and fuss over.

Speaking of babies, a few years after Ryan and Kelly were married, they were blessed with a son, Riley Ethan. We called Riley the miracle child because a "well-meaning" physician told them it was impossible for them to have any children. Well, God had other ideas and when man makes his dogmatic proclamations, it's just like our all-knowing heavenly Father to intervene and remind him who is in control. Sure, Kelly took extra precautions, followed her doctor's instructions religiously, and prayed a lot. In fact, we all prayed and asked the Lord to protect both Kelly and the little baby on the way. Can you imagine our elation and thanksgiving to God when this beautiful baby boy was born?

The birth of a child is truly a miracle—a miracle in which God gives parents an opportunity to cooperate with Him in His creating process. One Bible scholar aptly called a mother's womb, "the laboratory of God." I have heard many doctors make similar statements. I believe that the reproductive process in all creatures is a miracle of the Lord. Those who cannot see this are missing one of the greatest wonders of God's creation.

After Kelly and Ryan and their new "bundle of boy" were settled in for a while, Brenda and I made a visit to see the little guy. Of course I was curious to find out how Pudge was reacting over this tiny "intruder." That is how cats often view a baby or someone who comes into "their" domain. Well, they were glad to report that Pudge didn't resent the new arrival and was handling the change in a very mature way. Many times pets are as excited as their humans are over an addition to the family, whether it is an addition the normal and natural way, an adoption, a foster child, or some other means. To the pet, this is someone else to shower with love and affection, and also, another person from whom to receive attention.

Now Pudge was a country cat and used to having some space. Living in town, she was restricted because of the many hazards of city life. Ryan and Kelly took precautions to protect her and monitored her whereabouts if she was on the back porch. But one day, Pudge got out and disappeared for a couple of days. It is not strange for a cat to explore; it's in their nature to satisfy their curiosity. However, this was not the right environment for a feline to be wandering around in seeing the sights.

Knowing my love for and interest in cats, Kelly called to notify me of the situation, and I immediately put Pudge on our private prayer list. We prayed for her safe return, being well aware of the dangers she would face on the streets. One of these dangers is epitomized by a bumper sticker I saw on a pickup truck in Sunbury one day. I was following the truck through town and at a red light I noticed the sticker which read: I Love Cats. Under those big, bold letters were some smaller words in parenthesis. I craned my neck to read them before the light changed. I was appalled and angered. These words read: (dead ones). What a sick mind, I thought. If the driver shared those sentiments, he needs help. Unfortunately, there are many cruel and callous individuals out there who, for whatever psychotic reason, seem to take morbid pleasure in killing or hurting animals. They, too, need our prayers. I am not referring to the sport of hunting, farming, or raising stock for food. The Bible sanctions these and so do I. It is the deliberate acts of cruelty that I condemn.

Our prayers were answered! Kelly called to tell me that Pudge was home and showed no visible signs of injury or trauma. After a two day extravaganza on the town, Miss Pudge returned offering no explanation. I'm sure that Ryan and Kelly did not demand one, but were just glad that she was back safe and sound. We all were! And the little feline senior citizen continues to be part of the Heim household.

"MR. BUD"

The next cat I wish to tell you about lives quite a distance away in Ann Arbor, Michigan. He is known as Bud or "Mr. Bud" by his person, Barbara Deroba, the daughter of one of our Zion Church members, Thelma Deroba. Although I have never "met" Mr. Bud, I feel that I know him through conversations with Thelma and especially through correspondence with Barbara.

Bud came into Barbara's life when a neighbor moved from the area and did not want the responsibility of taking him to a new place. She has always liked animals and was willing to give this orange "Morris-look-alike" a home, being aware of the extra work it would involve. She knew that he was used to a litter box and was well past the kitten stage, so there wouldn't be too much ripping and tearing throughout her house. He would be good company for her and vice versa.

Like most cats, Mr. Bud is an "independent dependent." However, this male chauvinist thinks that Barbara should be at his beck and call, walk three feet behind him, and address him as "Mister." He has the ludicrous idea that he is in charge of the household and that everything revolves around him and his wants and needs. If Barbara does not respond as quickly as he thinks she should, he resorts to nipping her on the leg. I told Thelma that perhaps he was like some men who think women are a step below the male species. If he did, he was in for a surprise.

Now Barbara is not a woman's libber; she does not hate men, nor does she consider herself to be in a contest or competition with the opposite sex. She has a good attitude toward all people in general and is willing to go the extra mile for anyone. She is intelligent, loving, understanding, kind, and patient. However, she was not about to pushed around by a pompous pussycat, male or female. Bud was going to have to give a little and make some adjustments to her rules. This was not going to be a one-sided relationship.

Well, Mr. Bud did not like Barbara's attitude at all, but he soon realized that she was not going to do all the giving in, and he began to mellow. Sure, like any cat, he is still somewhat demanding and presumptuous, but he has made a few concessions. Let's just say that he and Barbara have come to a feline/human understanding.

One evening when Brenda and I were visiting with Thelma, she told us of some of her daughter's adventures with the kitty. Barbara is quite ingenious and she figures out methods to handle whatever situations arise. One of these deals with having to give Mr. Bud a cat medication, something every cat owner faces at one time or another. Since Bud is an older cat, Barbara has found it necessary to administer various forms of medicine to him more often.

The best way she found to give her cat his medication is to lay him over on his back on the floor and straddle him with her legs. This method prevents him from getting away and helps protect her from the struggling feline. So far, Barbara has been successful in getting the proper dosages in the kitty.

Bud has had his problems over the years, with pancreatitis, some teeth pulled, and constipation. More recently, he hasn't been able to retract his claws so he gets stuck on things. Barbara has been calling him her "sticky budder." With all of Bud's adventures, or misadventures, I told Barbara that she should write a book about him. She said that she knew what the title would be: "Bud, A Stand-Up Guy!"

"TIGGER"

Another of our couples, Jim and Peggy Deroba, have a dark grayish black tiger cat by the name of Tigger. We first met this very friendly kitty when we visited Peggy and Jim in their home in nearby Bloomsburg. Brenda and I always like to make new feline friends and Tigger was a fine host and gentleman. He accommodated us with our oohing and aahing over him and seemed to eat it up. Jim said, "Don't talk baby-talk to him; he'll expect it from us." We laughed and went right on making much ado about the pussycat.

Jim is a high school teacher and has confiscated laser-wands from several students. These wands can be dangerous if not used properly and are not allowed to be in the student's possession in Jim's school. Now Jim has one of these wands, and he showed us how Tigger loves to chase the red dot emitted by the laser's light. Peggy said, "It will keep him entertained for quite a while." Jim added, "He just can't quite figure out why he is unable to pick it up when he does catch it." As we watched him go after the red dot, we saw that Tigger gave it his best effort.

On one occasion when we went to visit Peggy and Jim, we asked Sandy Ritchie, Peggy's mother and also a St. Elias member, to ride along with us. Peggy and Jim didn't know that Sandy was coming with us, and Jim wasn't home from school when we got there. Each time Sandy came up to their home, she would bring some of Peggy's belongings. It became a running joke between Sandy and Jim, as she would try to see how much stuff she could get in her car and Jim would ask, "Okay, what did you bring this time?"

True to form, when Jim arrived and saw Sandy, he asked, "What did you bring along this time?" We all laughed and Jim knew that Brenda and I had been clued in on the game. Sandy would usually come back with something like, "Well, it's Peggy's stuff so why should it be taking up space in my house?" Sounds logical to me!

Sandy is a widow. Her husband, Jerry, died eight years ago at the young age of fifty-four. She still maintains their farm and remains a member of three antique auto clubs. Jerry's hobby was collecting and restoring Model-T and Model-A Fords. He had five completely restored and was working on some more. Her son, Mark, is currently working on a 1929 Franklin. Like the rest of us, Sandy likes Tigger and gets a kick out of watching him be a cat. I told her at church one day that Tigger was her "grandcat," since Peggy and Mark did not have any children as yet. She did not mind that appellation, but found it quite cute. (Of course, Brenda and I tell our mothers that they are Taffy and Tiffy's grandparents.)

However, Sandy was elated to give us some news later on that Peggy and Jim were expecting. When Elizabeth was born, I for one, was curious how Tigger reacted to their new addition to the family. Well, he was fascinated with this little "person" and took an unusual interest in her care. Jim told us that Tigger appointed himself as Elizabeth's personal guardian. He wanted to be wherever she was, and at night, he took up vigil by her crib. Many times cat owners do not know what their pet's reaction to a baby will be. It is cause for serious concern especially since most cat people love their pets and are quite attached to them. In Tigger's case, things worked out well and that is what everyone hoped for.

A few years later, Mark and his wife, Debbie, announced that they were expecting parents, and soon, a son, Eric, was born. I told Sandy, "A granddaughter, a grandson and a grandcat—you are very blessed." She agreed!

"FROSTY"

One of our St. Elias members, Helen Chere, has a ball watching her daughter Cleo's cat, Frosty, when she visits them in the Poconos in northeast Pennsylvania. The Pocono Mountains are beautiful and a great tourist attraction for vacations and honeymoons. Cleo and husband, Jerry, have a home nestled in these gorgeous rolling mountains. They are surrounded by the beauty and wonders of nature, and it is here that Frosty is entertained by a plethora of wildlife.

One of Frosty's best buddies is a gray squirrel who began coming to the deck on the back of the house looking for handouts. At first, Frosty tried to chase this intruder on her turf, but the little beggar was persistent and eventually won the kitty over. As Helen related to me, the two are a blast to watch as they communicate and play through the patio door and screen.

Helen told me that Frosty loves to travel with Cleo and Jerry to Snead's Ferry, North Carolina, for the annual Shrimp Festival. The locals make the event into a real gala affair which attracts visitors from all over the country. Frosty, so named because of her gray, white and tan long hair that gives a "frosted" effect, loves the area, the shrimp, and the little lizards that go darting around the seashore. She is fascinated by these little creatures that move so quickly and are an inviting quarry to chase. Although I have yet to meet Frosty, I can picture her in my mind's eye, playing with her friend the squirrel, piggin' out on shrimp, and lazin' in the North Carolina sun leapin' on lizards.

"ALLIE"

Another of our St. Elias couples, Grant and Holly Renninger and their daughter, Casey, have a delightful little female cat named Allie. While visiting them one evening, Brenda and I had the pleasure of meeting this adorable light gray kitty. Of course, I began calling her "Alley Cat," thinking of the reference to strays that frequented the alleys of our cities in bygone days. Casey got a kick out of this, listening to this old duffer tell tales of times and adages years before she was born. I haven't quite accepted my senior citizen status, often forgetting just how old I am. My young wife doesn't let me lose sight of the fact that I am closing in on seven decades and takes great pleasure in reminding me of my antiquity. I always tell her that her day is coming.

As the evening went on, we were thoroughly entertained by Alley, who at this time, was a kitten and full of the usual vim and vigor. Grant and Holly have sectional couches, and there are gaps or spaces between them. The frolicking kitty would reach up through them and bat at us without notice. Casey told us that this was one of Alley's favorite tricks, trying to surprise you when you least expected it. She made sure that there was never a dull moment.

A couple summers ago, we were preparing for Vacation Bible School and had a work day at the church. As we were feasting away on pizza and lasagna, Holly told us of a parrot that showed up in their backyard some time ago. As she described the little feathered creature, Kelly spoke up and said that the bird closely resembled her Dad's parrot that recently flew the coop. The description was too vivid to be a coincidence.

Well, Holly and Casey's hearts sank because they knew what they had to do, and they had become attached to "Larry" as Casey called the parrot. Someone had a cell phone, and Holly called Rudy and his wife, Debbie, to inform them of the vagabond bird. To the delight of Casey and Holly, and really all of us, Rudy and Debbie told them to keep the parrot who apparently was not happy at their home. In fact, Debbie came down to the church with a cage, books, food, and some other items to give Casey. We all thought that was a nice gesture.

It was nice to see Casey and Holly so elated over this happy turn-about. I'm such a pushover for happy endings and seeing people do nice things for people. I thank the Lord whenever I hear about acts of kindness, and I am especially grateful when I see them first hand. We all should try to do something nice for someone every day. What a difference it would make!

I was glad to hear that Allie accepted her new friend and was not interested in making a meal out of the little cutie. It certainly is not a "Sylvester and Tweetie" relationship. And by the way, Casey learned that the parrot's name was "Ginger." Somehow, "Larry" just doesn't seem to fit.

"KITTEN"

Two of the nicest people I have ever met are owned by a feline named "Kitten." Homer and Phyllis Klock are members of our St.

Elias Church and are very dedicated to the Lord. Actually, Homer was born and raised on the farm across the road from the church and his family was very involved in its ministry. St. Elias used to be shared by people of the Lutheran and Reformed faith, and when the Lutheran Churches of the area united in one large church, Homer's family went with them. Living so closely to the church their family almost automatically became the caretakers, building fires in the old coal furnace, clearing away snow, doing some cleaning, and a host of other chores.

Homer's parents were deeply involved spiritually as well in the church and set a very good example for their children in the home. Besides being hard workers, they lived their Christian faith and gave no occasion to anyone to find fault. Homer often remarks that he is so thankful to God for the parents he was blessed to have.

Phyllis, too, was fortunate to have been raised in a Christian home and exposed to the life-changing principles of God's Word. She and Homer compliment each other beautifully and I am convinced that their 50 plus years of marriage was ordained by God. I would describe Phyllis as elegant, sophisticated, polished, and very pleasant to be around. If you are in her home, you will find her to be a most gracious host.

Now, do you get the idea that Kitten is a very lucky kitty? Well, of course, I do not believe in luck, but rather the providence of God. I believe that our loving Lord brings people into each other's lives and that He does the same with people and pets. I am convinced that He brought Kitten to Homer and Phyllis, and a great relationship has developed.

This pretty gray and white tiger with a dark nose revels in their company and enjoys being part of the family. She is not really a lap cat, but sometimes she jumps up to be loved and petted. After spending some time on the back porch, and especially if it is cold, Kitten likes a warm lap to curl up on. Phyllis is usually the choice and it matters little to Kitten if the lady of the house is doing something or not. Like most cats, she expects to be catered to immediately.

At night, Kitten sleeps with Phyllis mainly because Homer has some back problems and does not stay in one position. Phyllis does not move about much at all and that suits Kitten just fine. She sleeps on a special pad that Phyllis made for her and keeps to this arrangement on a consistent basis. One day, Phyllis said to Homer that Kitten must have been upset with her because she slept in Sam's bed downstairs. Sam, really Samantha, is their daughter's Greyhound, who spends time with them when Marilyn is at work or away. Marilyn and her daughter, Erika, live right next door, so the pets are well-acquainted and get along fine.

Sam, the Greyhound, is a retired race dog who has an amicable disposition, and Kitten appreciates that laid-back approach to life as most cats do. Marilyn and Erika have cats as well and provide a nice home for them and Sam. It should be very evident that Kitten and her counterparts are the recipients of a lot of love and care in these fine Christian homes. Marilyn is also a member at St. Elias and like her parents, is dedicated to the Lord. I thank Him every day for people like Homer and Phyllis and Marilyn who make my job easier and my ministry worthwhile. I also thank Him for their pets!

"VARIETY AND LOVE"

Cats have many things in common and there are characteristics identical to all felines. However, there are differences as well. Both sides can be seen in the cats I have mentioned in this chapter. Our four-footed furry little pals do not all like the same things. Most cats seem to like catnip, although Taff and Tiff do not; some enjoy table scraps, others don't; some do not mind water (getting wet), others do; while lots of kitties love to see company come to visit in their homes, many are frightened and intimidated by their presence. The comparisons go on.

Cat lovers delight in sitting down and sharing stories about their pets. These cat tales include side-splitting accounts of hilarious situations, nerve-racking incidences of danger, and heart-warming episodes of love and devotion. They never cease to amuse and amaze us with their almost-human characteristics. I am sure this is what God had in mind when He created them and sent them into our lives.

In this wonderful world of wonders, God has created variety, or diversity, if you will. This variety extends to mankind and animals, and who is not at least somewhat awed by our Lord's creative imagination? Paul, the Apostle, tells us in Acts 17:26:

And He made from one man's blood every nation of mankind to settle upon the entire face of the earth.

When we look at the various races of the world, we cannot but be impressed with the different colors and features of people around the globe. There are hundreds of languages spoken by the inhabitants of this earth, multitudes of traditions and beliefs, and countless other categories of dissimilarities. Yet, the Bible tells us that God created them all from one man's blood.

What about the animals? Moses tells us that God created them, forming many different species in Genesis 1:25:

And God created the animals according to their kind.

How many different animals exist on this great planet of ours? One source I consulted reports that there are over 900,000 kinds of animals in the world. No wonder it took man so long to find, study, and classify them.

How about cats? There are many varieties of cats today due to cross-breeding. The most popular breed still seems to be the domestic short-hair. People looking for a pet will have an ample amount of different cats to choose from.

As you read this chapter you no doubt were also touched by the love between the people and their pets. From the cat's side, the love is mostly unconditional. They are not usually concerned if we look like a movie star or are rich and famous. They accept us as we are. We should be more like them. Nathan the Prophet told King David a story about a poor man who had a little female lamb, the only animal he owned. The story, found in 2 Samuel 12, says in verse three:

....He raised it, and it grew up with him and his children. It ate his food, drank from his own cup, and slept against his chest, and was like a daughter to him."

This is the kind of love you find between individuals and their pets, and especially as I have found, between cats and the people who love them. God help us to have this same love for each other!

CHAPTER 2

OH, THAT TAFFY!

For those of you who have not yet read about our two parsonage cats, Taffy and Tiffany came into our lives almost 15 years ago and have been close to our hearts ever since. As you will see through some of the stories in this book, each one is unique and has their own special place in our lives.

The title to a popular song of years ago, "Can't Help Falling in Love With You," somewhat expresses the affection Brenda and I have for Taffy. We both have said it: There is just something about Taffy that draws you to her, that makes you want to pick her up and love her. We can't explain it, but we know that people and pets alike have this effect on us and others, too. There are certain individuals and animals that have that special something that attracts you to them. Taffy seems to have that "special" quality.

After people had read the original *Cats in the Parsonage,* we had a lot of cat lovers who reinforced our own feeling about Taff— they would like to meet her and give her hugs and kisses. They were intrigued by the aura of this little cat who carried herself as if she knew she was here for a purpose. Brenda and I are convinced that she is. As you read this chapter about her, make your own deduction.

THE NAP
One evening after supper I promised this remarkable kitty that

I would take a little nap with her before going visiting. The next day, ironically, the eight cartons of my first book arrived at the parsonage. That great event in my life helped me remember the day as well. Aren't we creatures of association?

Well, I had two interruptions after making that promise to Taffy, which was, "Tassy, Daddy has to do something and then I will be up and lay down with you in the spare bedroom." I was on the stairway landing when I gave my word as a gentleman, and the kitty abruptly turned and ran into the spare bedroom and jumped up on the bed. I crept up the steps and peeked in at her and she was meowing profusely. I repeated my promise and descended the stairway to finish my chores.

A short while later, I started back up the steps and Taff was again waiting at the top, reminding me of my agreement in no uncertain terms. As I stopped on the landing, I remembered another thing that demanded my attention, and I once more reiterated my pact with the pussy cat. She again sped into the spare bedroom and up onto the bed.

I went back downstairs to take care of the pressing need and completed it as quickly as I could. I knew that little Miss Multi-Colored would be waiting, and I hurried back up. Before I even reached the landing, I heard her meows, and as I turned the corner, there was da' Tass impatiently walking from one side to the other, scolding me for my breach of promise. I apologized to my little sweetie who did an about-face and in a flash was on the spare bed. Just then I remembered something else I had to attend to and excused myself with, "Taffy, I'll be right back. Daddy promises!" And I went downstairs feeling like the "white man" making and breaking all those treaties with our native American Indians.

Soon I was on my way back up the stairs, thinking that Taff forgot about my promise or just gave up on the paleface who spoke with a forked tongue. As I rounded the corner, I was almost embarrassed to make eye-contact with her. Maybe, I thought, she won't be there. Fat chance! She was there, but this time the Kitty was silent. Sitting at the top of the stairway, she just stared at me with those big dark eyes. She didn't look away; she never made a sound; she just continued to look me square in the eyes. Only Taffy has this nerve-shattering stare!

It seemed like an eternity. My guilt was almost more than I could bear. I felt like dropping to my knees and making a confession. I could feel the perspiration forming on the back of my neck. I was sure that I was having palpitations. I....wait a minute! What am I doing? She's only a cat! Only a cat? I knew that I didn't feel that way about Taffy. It wasn't the first lie I told myself. I was so engrossed in the moment that I didn't hear Brenda come up behind me. Being the wise wife and mommy that she is, she surmised the situation and then said, "Well...Pinocchio?" I almost wet my pants!

My spouse thought that startling me was hilarious, not to mention that the kitty had me in a very vulnerable position. "She is very good at making you feel guilty, isn't she?" Brenda asked.

I answered, "Yes she is, and you're not helping the situation by encouraging her."

My "other half" came back with, "I didn't do anything. This is between you and Taffy. Now, are you going to lie down with her or not?" I looked back up the steps. The pussycat in question had not moved. She was still glaring at me, keeping silent, not moving a hair.

I managed to utter, "Tassy, do you still want to lay down with Daddy?" The Kitty meowed, ran into the spare bedroom, and jumped up on the bed. I apologized over and over to her, and all was forgiven.

After the nap, as I was getting ready to go visiting, I said to Brenda, "Do you believe that? What doesn't Taffy understand that we are saying to her?"

My soul-mate laughed, "We will have to be careful what we say in her hearing." Although we were kidding, we had some reservations about our future conversations.

THE WAKE-UP CALL

We continue to be amazed at Taff and Tiff's understanding. To keep from giving things away when we didn't want them to be alerted to what we were doing, believe it or not, we began spelling words out. For example, one of us would say, "Did you give the kids their t-u-n-a?" In a flash one or both of them would be there meowing for their treat. Maybe spelling out the word tuna sounds similar to saying it, but it is still scary.

Vet is another word we started to spell and perhaps it is the same situation as with tuna. Nevertheless, when we spell the word v-e-t, the girls become mysteriously scarce. Of course, if we happen to mistakenly rattle one of their pet taxis, they go into hiding. Packing a suitcase can bring about the same results.

Some other words having to do with their medications comprise more terms that we spell out if we remember in time. We continually shake our heads or give each other a dumbfounded look when we think about our behavior around the cats. Brenda once commented, "It's like having children in the house. You have to watch everything you say." Parents have learned to talk in code to prevent their kids from hearing things for various reasons. Living in Pennsylvania, I am familiar with a dialect known as Pennsylvania Dutch. I have heard quite a few folks from that background say that their parents spoke in Dutch if they didn't want them to understand the conversation. Many times it had to do with a serious situation, and the parents wanted to spare the children any needless concern. I cannot say that is the reason Brenda and I try to "talk around" our kitties, but we do it sometimes because we do not want to cause them unnecessary trauma. Most of the time we just have a lot of fun trying to outsmart them. We don't always succeed.

All of the preceding is to lead up to a cute little episode that took place one September. Due to acid reflux and some other digestive problems, up to five nights a week I sleep in my recliner downstairs. (I have made several trips to the Gastroenterology Department in a local hospital. I am thankful, though, because I could have more serious problems.)

That morning around 4:00 a.m., my thoughtful spouse decided to send a wide-awake Taffy down to keep me company. The kitty had been prancing from one end of the bed to the other, purring and semi-meowing, demanding some attention from a sleepy and uncooperative Mommy. Brenda repeated to her several times, "Taffy, go downstairs and sleep with Daddy." Soon, I was awakened by a pumped-up pussycat who jumped up on my lap.

Now since it wasn't my morning to get up at 4:00 a.m., I tried to persuade this pulsating ball of fur to lie down and sleep some more. After a while, she gave in and actually stayed with me until about 5:30 when she heard Brenda's radio come on upstairs. Then it was back to see what Mommy was doing and off she went to grace Brenda with her presence. I decided to arise myself and learned that my wife was the culprit in encouraging Taffy to come down and spend some quality time with her Daddy. I was not upset in the least and, once again, we both agreed that our kitties understood much more than we were aware of.

THE KISS

Our version of Miss Kitty, the feisty saloon owner in the long running western series, "Gunsmoke" 1956-1975, had a problem with her backside. The technical designation is "anal sac expression," and I'm sure that most cat owners have experienced this situation with their pets. Although it is not a serious condition, it is discomforting to the cat. As concerned "parents," Brenda and I called our good friend at the Sunbury Animal Hospital and, of course, they told us to bring Taffy right over.

Dr. James Temple was on duty that day, and he explained our kitty's problem to us. Dr. Temple sees patients of all sizes, but he is also a traveling veterinarian, going out to farms to treat larger animals. I'm sure that he has some great stories to share during his tenure as a physician of God's wonderful creatures.

After examining his very compliant client, Dr. Temple relieved the kitty's annoying condition and gave us some instructions to follow to help alleviate her distress until the problem was corrected. The main procedure was to apply a warm compress 2-3 times a day, and this would make the soreness go away. (We did exactly as he instructed and soon the puddycat was back to normal.)

As we were about to put the little patient in her pet taxi and go home, Dr. Temple picked her up, nuzzled her face against his, and gave her a kiss on the cheek. Brenda was busy getting the pet taxi ready and didn't see what happened next, but I did! After Dr. Temple kissed her on the cheek, Taffy turned her little head and looked him right in the face with one of the strangest expressions I have every seen. Her eyes were so big and open wide that I could tell we had here a totally surprised kitty cat. To my knowledge, no one but Brenda and I had ever kissed the Tassers on the cheek. She was completely caught unaware and it showed on her face. I wish I had it on video tape.

The kiss didn't assuage all of Taffy's fears of being at the vet's, but she didn't exactly run into her pet taxi either. Once in the taxi, however, she gazed up at Dr. Temple, this guy who stole a kiss, still with a look of surprise and a little bit of wonder. For the time being, Taffy realized that she was safe and that this man cared about her and meant her no harm. And Brenda and I appreciate the compassionate concern and attention that Dr. Temple and the other veterinarians give Taff and Tiff and, I'm sure, the many pets they treat. May God bless them and reward their efforts.

THE PURPLE BALL INCIDENT

Not long after I completed Cats I, Taffy amazed us with her uncanny perception and, I suspect, some feline sense of humor. As I have stressed before, this is one incredible cat. Sometimes I think that she understands 90 percent of what we say to her. That would be remarkable but I also know what a remarkable God we have as our heavenly Father, and He created her.

Brenda had purchased some toy balls that are furry and have a squishy center. They come four in a pack and are all different colors: yellow, green, pink and purple. For various occasions, like Christmas and birthdays, we bought some more of these balls so the kids had 16 of them. Taff especially loves them and plays with them incessantly. We find them all over the house, even downstairs, which makes us think that the multi-colored kitty makes her rounds after we are in bed.

One evening Brenda and I were upstairs playing with Taff and Tiff and decided to locate all the furry balls. Quite a feat when you consider where a cat can send a ball while they are batting them around. We have found them everywhere! Finding all of these furry toys has become quite a challenge and we get a kick out of seeing the cats "watch" us look for them. They even look under the bed and other furniture with us as if trying to help.

On this particular night, we were able to locate 15 of the 16 and put them in their toy basket. Only one purple ball was missing. We were ready to go downstairs and join Mary (Brenda's mother who lives with us) for a time of relaxation before turning in, and then I decided to give Taffy some instructions. They went something like this: "Taffy, Mommy and Daddy are going downstairs for a while. When we come back up to bed, you had better have found that purple ball." Well, Taffy sat there in the spare bedroom watching and listening with what I call "swept-winged" ears, not flat, but pointed out to each side. She looked somewhat confused and hurt as if I was reprimanding her, so I said softly, "Tassy, find that ball."

We left the room and descended the stairs still being eyed by the kitty as we went. As is Tiffany's habit, she followed us down and jumped up on Brenda's lap where she stayed until we went to bed. After getting her Mother ready and settled in for the night, my wife and I went upstairs, not really remembering what we had in-structed Taffy to do. Brenda headed for the bedroom and I went into the "kids" room to clean the litter box. Then came a near blood-curdling scream from our bedroom.

"Cllllaaaaiiirrrrr!!!!!!" I stopped what I was doing and hurried over to the bedroom. My partner said not a word but pointed to the bed where in the center of the cover lay…a purple ball! It couldn't have been placed there more perfectly. It was nearly dead-center in the middle of the bed. We stood there stunned, amazed in disbelief. Brenda turned and looked down the hallway and touched my shoulder. There was Miss Multi-Colored sitting in the spare bed-room doorway staring at us with what I swear was a proud smirk.

We were speechless! Finally, I managed to say in a squeaky voice, "Tasssssss!" The little stinkpot turned and slowly walked back into the room. Her expression was like unto a smart aleck "Ha! Ha!" It wasn't the first time she had outwitted us, especially me, her pastor-daddy. This is one intelligent pussycat!

I had to know! Was it the missing ball or one out of the basket? I went over to the spare bedroom and Brenda followed me. I sat on the floor in front of the toy basket and counted the balls. There were four green, four yellow, four pink, and three purple! I looked up at Brenda who was standing in the doorway staring at the four clusters of furry balls on the floor—15 balls! We both glanced around at Taffy who was sitting across the room in front of the crib, gloating over her victory and looking at us as if to say, "What did you expect to find?" The little tyke then smugly turned and went under the crib and into her small pet taxi, curled up, and ignored us.

"She knew exactly where that ball was," Brenda said. "I know she did, the little brat," I replied. My wife then tossed the fourth purple ball into the toy basket and we retired for the night, chuckling over the incident but still in awe about our kitty. We still are amazed by what happened and love to share the story with others.

The folks at both our churches laughed hysterically as I related the account, and the cat lovers nodded in agreement, knowing what it is to be outsmarted by a feline. Of course, my parishioners love to see their pastor outdone, especially by Taffy who always keeps things exciting and interesting around the parsonage.

God has placed a very competent brain in the cat's head for their benefit and ours. We are still learning about our two little gifts from the Lord. He knows that we need these little episodes in our lives to give us a wake up call, to make us aware of the greatness of His creatures, and to lighten us up a bit. As we went to bed that evening and prayed together, we said, "Heavenly Father, thank you for the Taffers!"

CAM-CORDER CAT

Brenda and I do not yet own a camcorder, and I thought it would be nice to have the cats on a movie video. So we borrowed one from Ed and Joanna Hovenstine, a couple in our St. Elias Church. I understand that recently their daughter, Missy, got a kitty and now we have another cat lover in our charge. Missy and her brother, Kramer, keep Ed and Joanna busy with sports and other school activities, so we did not want to tie up the camera too long. We used it for a couple months in the summer, getting it back to them before the school events were in full swing. Again, I have to say how grateful we are to our people who go out of their way to accommodate us.

I have to share here an amusing story about Joanna's mother, Leona Raker, also a member of St. Elias. Joanna's dad, Donald, went home to be with the Lord after a six year battle with multiple myloma, a cancer of the blood. We miss this wonderful man who loved the Lord and who was such a pleasure to be around.

Well, one evening after Donald had passed away, Brenda and I were visiting with Leona in her home right off Route 890. I had always complimented Donald and Leona on their nice house, built and furnished with excellent taste. They achieved two great characteristics of a house I think most people desire: a sense of homeyness and class! It's on my list of one of the finest homes around. The setting is nice, too, with a woods right behind the backyard providing them with colorful scenery and a variety of wildlife.

One of the frequent visitors from the woodland that Leona sees is what I call a "two-toned pussycat with fluid drive." Of course, I am referring to a skunk whose species, I understand, is of no relation to the cat. If Taff and Tiff could speak English, I'm sure that they would inform me that they bear no kin to this perfidious perfume artist who can leave a putrid calling card that will pervade the air for days. Our hostess was telling us that these black and white visitors were making regular appearances around her house. We three concurred that they seemed to be getting bolder, venturing closer to homes and entering into towns and cities. They are increasingly becoming the victims of "road kill." In fact, several jokes have arisen due to this repeated occurrence. One goes like this:

"Why did the chicken cross the road?
"To show the skunk and the possum it can be done!"

Now, I do not like to see animals killed on the road, and when I am driving I do my best to avoid harming any of them. I do not find it amusing when I see an animal dead along the highway. However, the skunk's proclivity to cross the thoroughfare so filled with speeding automobiles along with his miserable record of failures does make one wonder about his navigational skills.

With this in mind, Brenda and I were traveling up 890 some evenings later and, lo and behold, we nearly hit a skunk crossing the road. Brenda said, "Wow! That looks like a fat mama, and she's heading toward Leona's." The large, possibly pregnant pole cat, went up the steep bank after reaching the other side safely and did head somewhat in the direction of Leona's hacienda. My teasing wife then kidded, "I'm going to tell Leona to keep her skunks at home!" As I recall, Leona later informed Brenda that they were not her skunks!

Well, back to the camcorder. Ed gave us a quick course on how to use the camera and we didn't do too badly with it. I'm not about to apply to Warner Brothers or any other movie studio for a cameraman's job, but we did okay and are pleased with our tape. I am amazed at the technology in these little machines providing you with sight and sound. We kept checking the tape to see what we were getting and we were pleased with the sharpness.

Taffy wasn't quite sure about this thing that Mommy and Daddy were holding up in front of their faces, but after we also used our regular camera on an alternate basis, she didn't seem to be wary of it anymore. As I reported in Cats I, both of our girls are hams and like to pose for pictures, Taffy being the bigger show-off. I am sure that they do not fully comprehend what we are doing, even though their eccentric parents show them photos of themselves and let them watch the video.

It's a blast to watch them look at the tape and wonder how this is all going on. They sit or lay on the bed in our bedroom, and seem to be fascinated with observing themselves on the TV. Of course, we encourage them with exclamations like, "Pretty Kitty," or a bunch of "ooh's" and "aah's," and "There's Tassy," or "There's Tissy." We just wonder what they are thinking.

We taped them in about every room upstairs and had to follow them around on various occasions as cats have their own agenda. Most of the time Miss Hamboat Taffy was cooperative, and we have her on film playing with her puffs and furry balls on the bed or in the bathroom especially. Miss Multi-Colored loves the bathroom and enjoys hopping in the tub or playing with Daddy on the floor.

One night after we came home from visiting, I went upstairs and was met at the top of the steps by a meowing three-colored cat. I am not sure what she was telling me, but I do know that it was important to her. She ran ahead of me into the bedroom and jumped up on the bed. I quickly grabbed my Kodak® camera and tossed a ball to Taffy, all the while egging her on to play. She ignored all of my attempts to get her to bat the ball or jump up to catch one of her puffs. The kitty just sat there looking straight into the camera, purring profusely and sporting a look of ecstasy on her face. Nothing I could do would entice the pussycat to budge from her spot on the bed.

All of this only took a few minutes and I am sure I forgot to turn the camera on in all my anticipation. As I was trying to coax the little nut to perform for me, all of a sudden I realized that she was not in the least bit interested in doing any tricks. She kept mixing her meows with her purring, which produces sort of guttural sounds, and rocking back and forth from side to side in an excited manner. All my pleading fell on deaf ears. The kitty continued her ritual.

Then Taffy ran to the end of the bed, still purring and mowling, and looked straight at the TV. At first I payed no attention and continued to try to get her to play. But after she repeated this several times, old slow daddy finally understood that his furry friend was trying to tell him something. She would run to the center of the bed and "pose" almost nervously, and then dash to the foot of the bed, stare at the television, and look back to me. I must have been a picture of total surprise, if anyone would have seen me, with gaping mouth and wide eyes. I managed to utter, "You want me to show you the video, don't you?" I was answered by a clear, resounding Meow!

"Brrrrrenda!" My wife came charging up the steps to see what the emergency was all about. I feebly tried to explain what was going on with the kitty, and Taffy, who had stayed on the bed, was still meowing and prancing from the middle to the foot, looking over at the TV. She did everything but point at it! "She wants to see the video," I said. My somewhat stunned spouse muttered softly, "I don't believe this cat." I was able to offer a mild rejoinder, "Neither do I."

What could we do? We popped the tape in the VCR and satisfied our kitty's desire. I have to admit, too, we enjoyed watching it again. Tiffy heard the voices on the tape and came running to join the fun. I looked at Brenda and said, "Never in a million years did I ever envision anything like this when we brought these cats in 13 years ago." She nodded in agreement. They continue to amaze us, especially Taffy—oh, that Taffy!"

A MESSAGE OF UNDERSTANDING

Probably the average pet owner doesn't give much thought to his cat, dog, or hamster trying to understand him. I never really did until Brenda and I adopted Taff and Tiff and we became engrossed in cats. I have read lots of books about them, including some technical ones that deal with their origin, their purring, and their peculiar behavior. I had done some reading on them when I bought my first Siamese, Tiffany, back in 1967, and learned that cats were very intelligent. Tiffany lived to be eleven and died of liver cancer in 1978. The Siamese is one of the most intelligent cats and I was often duped by Tiffany I. It was with her that I first became aware that cats observe and study us.

It must both astonish and confuse a cat when it watches one of us human beings. Given the curious creatures they are, it must boggle their minds trying to understand what we do and say. Many of us would agree that we have trouble understanding ourselves and other people much too often. Yet, God instructs us to seek to practice understanding along with other graces and virtues of the Holy Spirit. Note what the Apostle Paul says to us:

> *But rather in everything commending ourselves as God's servants...in purity, in understanding, in patient endurance, in kindness, in the Holy Spirit, in love without hypocrisy* (2 Corinthians 6:4,6).

Paul described how Christians are to commend themselves to others, that is, how they are to appear to people. Too often believers are abrasive and this harms the cause of the Lord Jesus to win all men to Himself. How desperately the world needs to see purity, to receive understanding and patience and kindness and sincere love, all produced in the child of God by the Holy Spirit. If any lasting good is to be accomplished in society, it is to be done through the saints of the Lord.

No doubt we have heard people say, "And we call them animals," referring to the terrible atrocities human beings perpetrate upon each other. A little understanding would go a long way. And here man can learn from the animals. In many ways they try to understand us and co-exist with us despite all our idiosyncrasies.

37

God's creatures are great teachers and good examples if we will see in them what He wants us to see.

Taffy and Tiffy have helped us immensely, and our Tassy especially has taught us to put forth some effort to understand, to be patient, and to be kind. She has fulfilled her mission from God, and that is one reason we will never forget her.

CHAPTER 3

TIFFANY, YOU LITTLE MONSTER!

Brenda and I have various names for our little buddies, as you may have already noticed from the previous chapters and from *Cats I*, if you read it. One of these came to be applied especially to Tiffany because of an incident one spring. Although Taffy usually steals the scene and is the predominant prankster, Tiffy has her moments. The following is one of them.

THE MIDNIGHT MONSTER

The Shaffer household normally goes to bed at a decent hour each night, but the turning-in time is often determined by the events of the next day. One particular evening we were up a little later than usual, and Brenda was the most tired of us three humans in the house. After helping her mother get ready for bed and taking care of pre-slumber necessities, my wife and I had our goodnight prayer, and she prepared for a nice sleep. I had a few things to attend to in the study before retiring to my recliner downstairs, so I was at my desk when I heard the noise.

I'm not sure where Taffy was that night, but I was certain that she was not responsible for the commotion. At first I had to listen closely because I had the door nearly shut, but soon I recognized the sound. The "Little One," as we refer to Tiffany, was playing with her brown monster. Now this brown monster looks like a furry shrunken head. It has two round, black eyes and a plastic box inside with a rattle. During the day when the kitty plays with it, the noise is not so distracting, but when one is trying to sleep in the quiet of the night, well…!

I also recognized the voice in the room next to me that sounded out in some displeasure. "Tiffanyyyyyy!" Silence! The quiet continued for a few minutes and then I detected that familiar rattle out in the hallway once more. Tiff must have picked up the monster in her mouth and shook it because the noise became more intense. She then batted it down the hallway right up to our bedroom door. The voice I know so well again expressed disapproval of the pussycat's playtime. "Tiffy, please go to sleep. Mommy's tired! Okay?"

Silence! Uh, huh! For a few minutes. Soon, I again heard the toy monster, this time being pushed into the bedroom. I waited for Brenda's reaction. It wasn't long in coming! "That's it! Tiffanyyyy— you little monster! Give me that! Look, monster's going to bed! So are you!" With that, the little fuzzy toy was put up out of the kitty's reach. My wife then peeked into the study. "Did you hear all of that?" she asked.

"All of what?" I inquired, acting innocently, trying not to laugh. "You know what," she retorted. "Why didn't you take it from her?"

I fumbled for an answer and finally decided on the truth. "Well," I said, "I thought it was cute, and I wanted to see how long you would let it go."

As she closed the door, my soul-mate replied, "I'm glad *you* thought it was cute. Don't be up too late."

Sometime later, Brenda found a green monster and bought it for Tiffany. It also has a rattle inside and this seems to fascinate Tiffers who took to it right away. These toys do not seem to interest Taffy in the least, as I have never seen her play with them. Now Tiff has two of them and that presented another problem, but more about that later.

TIFFY AND THE COPIERS

As a minister, I spend a lot of time in my study at the parsonage. Besides preparing messages and the Sunday bulletins, I answer letters and make lots of copies of various correspondence and church business. No! I do not use the same message at both churches that I pastor. In fact, each of the churches have their own order of service, so I print two different bulletins. I do not mind, I rather enjoy the diversity.

Pertaining to my messages, I like to work up and use a series, that is, a sequence of sermons on a given theme. The series may contain ten messages or as many as nineteen. They all contain positive solutions to the adversities of life, majoring on God's Word and the life-changing principles it teaches. The Bible is God's "How-To Manual" for life, and it contains the answers to all the problems we will face during our stay here on earth. If people would take the time to search its sacred pages, they would find effective, practical guidelines to help them in every area of their lives from eternal salvation to difficult life decisions. With the Holy Spirit's help, I hope to send my folks out the door on Sunday mornings feeling encouraged, inspired, and renewed. Right now, I am about six years ahead in my messages. Call me a control freak. I believe in preparation and organization, and no, I don't do it perfectly.

In my study, I have three copiers and I use all of them in my church work. One is a small personal copier that is slow and makes nine copies at a time and then stops. The medium-size copier is a lot faster and will print up to 99 copies at a clip. The larger machine is quite a bit more sophisticated, making 100 copies at a time at a fast pace, enlarging and reducing, serves as a printer for a computer, and will do a host of other functions. I certainly have not mastered all of its capabilities.

The two smaller copiers are older and operate with the top, or lid, shifting from right to left and back again as they make each copy. The larger copier is more advanced, and all movement takes place within the machine. One day, before I had the larger copy machine, I was using the small copier and I happened to notice that Tiffany had come into the study. She hopped up on the back of an arm chair I have in the room and sat there watching the copier. I chuckled as I observed her head go back and forth while the copier made its reprints. Each time it stopped, I would walk over and push the start button and begin the sequence again. Nine copies and stop!

I noticed that when the copier stopped, Tiff would look at me quite inquisitively as if to say, "Daddy, it quit!" Her ears were pointed outward, and she had that confused look on her face cats get when something has them baffled. If I needed more copies, I started it over again much to the kitty's delight. And she seemed content to sit and watch the copier as long as I made copies.

When we got the bigger copier, I thought Tiffer would not be interested since the lid did not move back and forth. However, after the new machine was in place, I was experimenting with it and she came in and hopped up on the armchair to observe. I had moved the medium-sized copier to another spot in the study and put the new one in its old place. I was surprised to see that she was as intrigued with this one as much as the others. The only movement this copier makes is when the paper comes out on the tray. But, for some reason, it attracts the kitty's attention. And, I am glad that she can derive some satisfaction from watching it.

THE SNACK TRAY

One day, I had left right after lunch to do some visiting and Brenda was about to clean up the dishes. We didn't have anything that day that we could give Tiffany, although little Miss Pest was right there begging for a tasty morsel. She seems to just want a sample of what you have to satisfy her curiosity. However, she will eat a good portion of hamburger, roast beef, and chicken from three well known fast-food restaurants respectively, if we let her! We know that too much of this kind of food is not good for her, or for us for that matter.

As Brenda removed the last item from her tray, she got a sudden surprise. Little impatient pussycat made her move! Like a flash she was up on the tray with all four feet planted squarely on the surface and did not tip it over. Now this was out of character for Tiffany because the cats are not allowed up on our tables or counters, or some other places. We trained them that way right from the start, and these two have been super in obeying our wishes. In fact, if we put them up some place where they are not normally allowed, they are very uncomfortable and try to get down. We are careful not to do this too often so that we do not confuse them. About the only place we put them up on a counter is the bathroom to check them over.

Well, as soon as Tiff was on the tray, she froze! She surprised herself and was partly frightened and, Brenda was certain, embarrassed! My wife said to the little culprit, "Well, young lady, what do you think you are doing?" Talk about being caught unawares. For a moment, the kitty didn't know what to do, but then she started to jump down. At that point, Brenda picked her up and loved her and reassured her that everything was all right. Then, she put the puddy-cat down and Tiff darted out of the room and up the steps. Mary said, "She knew she wasn't supposed to be up there." However, both ladies thought it was cute.

THE GREEN BALL

About the same time, we were getting ready for bed and Tiffany had been downstairs with us and had plopped on one of our laps as we watched TV. Since Taffy does not come down except to peek around the corner to see if Mary is still there, or to sneak out in the back room a while, Tiffy takes advantage of this time to be with Mommy and Daddy. The upstairs is "Taffy's world" and she is the predominant pussycat in that domain. Brenda and I know that we cater to the Taffers, but we do try to see that Tiff gets ample attention. I guess we feel that Taff is sort of being cheated out of having the run of her own home since we asked Mary to come and live with us. So we take extra care with the multi-colored kitty to compensate for her fears. Cats are complex creatures, and they make choices based on how they view reality. Taffy sees Mary as a threat; Tiffany does not. How we wish Taff would be more like her sister in this respect. And, are not we humans much the same as our kitty companions? Often we, too, have to live with the choices we make and put up with the resulting unpleasantries.

As we put the boob-tube to rest for the night, I said to Tiffany, "Okay, Tiff, let's go, it's time for bed. Uppy, uppy!" And with that, the little squirt jumped off my lap and ran ahead of me up the steps. Often, she will sit at the bottom and meow almost defiantly or run to the landing and sit there with much the same sassy cry. This time she went on up and when I rounded the corner, a green fuzzy ball came bouncing down to me. At the top of the steps was a "flat cat" with big dark eyes staring down at me. Tiff couldn't have gotten closer to the floor if she had been run over by a steam roller.

I heard Brenda in the hallway so I told her to quietly come up the stairs. She sneaked up to the landing and peeked around the corner and nearly lost it when she saw the low-lying kitty with fire in her eyes and ears flatter than a pancake. I showed her the ball on the landing and explained how it came bouncing down to me the minute I rounded the corner. Brenda said, "Tiffy set Daddy up real good, didn't she?" as she still watched the silent tense pussycat. "Does Tissy want to play ball?" my wife asked in baby talk. No movement from the furball. With that, she descended the staircase to finish getting Mary ready for bed.

I accommodated the little sweetie by tossing the ball up to her, much to the delight of the frisky feline. Now, Tiff hadn't yet learned to bat the ball back like her sister, but she went after it like gang-busters. When the ball reached her, she reared up with front feet flying and bounced it off the hallway wall. She was a furry blur of flighty motion as she managed to knock the ball back down to me. I tossed the ball back up to her and she repeated her frantic attempts to show this little green orb who was boss. She was one excited pussycat!

By this time, the other member of our feline family could no longer resist the temptation to investigate the commotion at the top of the steps. Mommy also came up to the landing, having finished her chores, and stopped beside me to surmise the situation. With the arrival of her multi-colored counterpart, Tiffany fled the scene assuming that we would now play with Taffy, an all-too-often occurrence. Feeling a bit guilty, we went on upstairs, located the slighted kitty and loved her up, telling her how well she played. Brenda advised, "We should do this more often." I nodded in total agreement.

NURSE TIFFANY

My doctor and hospital believe, after much testing, that I have a condition called Irritable Bowel Syndrome (IBS). Sometimes the condition causes severe pain in the abdomen similar to the misery of kidney stones. Right now there is no cure for IBS. I am on medication and an antacid, which I take after every meal and before going to bed. It can be annoying at times, but I thank the Lord that I do not have something more serious.

As I thought about this chapter on Tiffany, I recalled a flare-up of my condition one day. The pain hit me in the morning and was quite intense, doubling me up and showing no sign of stopping. My concerned wife called our doctor who advised using the antacid along with the medication. This episode was one of the worst, and as the severe pain decreased, I tried to lie down in the bedroom. Several times when I thought the occurrence was over and went to get up, the pain returned and caused me to stay put. I managed to doze off once in a while, but my internal disturbance kept reminding me that it was still there. Brenda checked on me at different intervals to see how I was doing and to offer some comfort. We both knew it just had to run its course.

Now the cats seem to sense when we do not feel well and often try to help in their feline way. Many times we have had two kitties curled up on each side of us when we were lying down because we were under the weather. They can somehow tell the difference between a nap and sickness. I again attribute this ability to our loving Creator who gives His creatures innate capacities to detect something is wrong. Both Taff and Tiff are sensitive to our health problems.

At this time Taffy was at the animal hospital being examined for a urinary obstruction and so Tiffany became "Nurse Kitty" for Daddy. She joined me in bed almost immediately, purring and meowing softly and looking at me with a sympathetic expression. The little squirt drew close to me on my right side and reached out with one paw and then the other to touch my cheek. Then she would inch back a bit and reach out and touch my chest or shoulder and look at me as if to say, "Did that help, Daddy?" I am continually amazed at our kitties' vast dimension of compassion.

I spent the rest of the morning in bed and opted to skip lunch due to my stomach distress. The ordeal continued into the afternoon and my little sweetie stayed faithfully at my side. She left only to eat or drink or use the litter box, and then returned to keep vigil with her ailing human. When she wasn't stroking me with a paw, she would lay her head on my arm or my chest. Her very presence was soothing and helpful as I waited for the IBS to subside. Near the end of this painful episode, Brenda came up again to check on me and commented on my on-duty nurse. I said, "She has been here the whole time, trying to make me feel better. She is a good little Florence Nightingale." After a kiss on the kitty's head, my partner went on about her household duties.

I had committed the experience to the Lord right from the beginning, realizing and accepting pain as a part of life on this old troubled earth. It was difficult, but I thanked Him for the pain as all Christians are to do: "Give thanks in all situations!" (I Thessalonians 5:18)

Yes, I wanted the pain to stop and I asked the Lord about this. And I kept remembering that pain is a good teacher and a reminder to be thankful for our many blessings. We tend to forget that when things are going well. I also gave thanks to my heavenly Father for our little cutie, Tiffany, who did her best to make me feel better. There sure is a lot of love present in that furry little scamp. Brenda and I know who put it there.

THE ILL-FATED KISS

One evening, I came home from visiting or a Confirmation Class (see how my memory is starting to fade in my senior years) and promptly got myself in trouble. I don't have much difficulty doing that, especially with my "other half." And my dilapidated memory plays a big part in getting myself in hot water.

I remember complaining about forgetting so much to one of my St. Elias members, Clyde Reitz, who was in his early nineties. "Clyde," I protested, "I can't remember stuff!" My dear friend eyed me for a moment and then said, "Clair...it gets worse!" I roared and couldn't wait to share this with his daughter, Barbara, and both congregations. Now, years later, I see what he meant. It has come miserably true!

Well, I came home from whatever I had been doing and went into the living room where I found Mary and Brenda in their recliners watching TV, and little Miss Tiffany was comfortably lying on an afghan spread over Mommy's lap. After saying hello to everyone, I walked over and kissed Tiffy on the head and then kissed Brenda. Did I make a mistake! Whoaaaaa! My hurt, but agitated wife let me know in no uncertain terms!

"You kissed Tiffy before you kissed me! Boy...I know where I stand!" Ever see a preacher lost for words? This one was! I couldn't think of a word to say. I tried to save myself by trying to lay some smooches on Brenda, but she wasn't about to play second fiddle. My romantic machinations got me nowhere. By this time, Mary was in hysterics, unable to contain herself. "Boy, Clair, you're in deep trouble now! You're going to have to work to get yourself out of this one," my mother-in-law insisted. My mischievous spouse continued to "act" angry and devastated, taking full advantage of the situation. And, of course, all of my excuses and explanations fell on deaf ears.

And Tiffany? With all the discussion and laughter going on, she became a bit frightened and took off upstairs. I followed after her and Brenda came along close behind. We didn't want the kitty to be traumatized because of our fun. She retreated to their house and was crouched down on the first floor when we found her, definitely confused and a little apprehensive. We managed to get her out and then consoled her with hugs and kisses, yes...kisses! And soon the purr-puppy was back downstairs on Mommy's lap, and then on mine, too. However, I did vow to myself to play it safe in the future and kiss the cat *after* kissing my wife.

"MOMMY, TIFFY SCUTCHED ME!"

When I first used the word "scutched," I wasn't sure it was a legitimate word. I couldn't find it in my thesaurus, but I did locate it in my *Webster's Seventh Collegiate Dictionary*, which defined the word scutch—to beat, to beat out, to strike. I was happy that it was a bona fide term so I could use it in the book. However, I have been known to coin a word or two if it suited my purpose. Sometimes my loving wife gives me one of her patented looks when she questions something I say. I smile and go on as if I know what I'm talking about.

Tiffany started "scutching" when still in the kitten stage, and Brenda and I were amused by this cute antic, most of the time! For some reason, perhaps known only to herself, our little furball would dart out from under the bed at breakneck speed just as we were walking by. This sudden acceleration was accompanied by a loud me-yyykk, sometimes uttered once or the entire distance down the hallway. At first, we thought she was having some sort of a fit or was in pain or that Taffy did something to her. But it seems the poo pot just likes to surprise you or scare you half to death. We agreed, it is hard to tell what lurks in the mind of a prankish and playful kitty cat. Tiffany still loves to pull this stunt even though she is now a "Grimalkin"—an old female cat. Although she is more than 16 years of age, she acts like a five or six year old cat. And, she is not really "old," since indoor cats live an average age of 15-25 years.

The little "Scutcher" also loves to wait until you start down the steps or start to go into the bathroom, and then she zooms down the hallway right behind you letting out some of those noisy me-yyykk's. If you are not expecting it, she can shock your system. And sometimes she doesn't make the me-yyykk sound when she thunders past you, but the result is about the same. Often when she pulls off a successful scutch, I will say, "Mommy, Tiffy scutched me! Brenda usually encourages the little duffer with, "Way to go, Tissy!" However, it's a different story when the kitty "gets" her! Then I hear warnings and threats of bodily harm to the furball, which only serves to encourage her even more.

I turned the pussycat's favorite prank into a game or a contest, trying to see if I could turn around and grab her before she got by me or say, "Gotcha!" As I started to go down the stairs, I would turn around very quickly, crouch down, and intercept the speeding tabby and bowl her over, gently, of course! The first time I did this, it totally surprised the Tiffers and I wish I had a picture of the look on her face. You would have thought she was down to her ninth life. Cats are proud creatures, and I had out-maneuvered my furry buddy with some flair. I thought perhaps it would ruin the game for her, but it seemed to just make her more determined not to get caught.

One of her new strategies was to sneak slowly part way down the hallway, speed up just as I took the first step down the stair-case, and plop on the floor behind me and roll around like a silly nut. The ensuing me-yyykk or me-yyykk's, being translated into

English, probably mean, "Gotcha, Dad!" I have to admit, she was very good at this and caught me unaware many times. It is amazing how cats can adjust to a problem or situation and figure out how to solve it or get around it. Just watch how they sit and stare at someone or something for long periods of time. Cat experts tell us that they are observing and processing the data in their feline minds, and are especially fascinated by us humans. I often wonder what they make of us, particularly our cruel side when we are more than less the people the Lord created us to be. How far we have fallen from His image! But, praise His name, we haven't totally effaced that image, there is still enough of it there to keep us from going totally berserk.

KITTY KARE? ISN'T THAT JUST LIKE GOD?

Sometime ago I read a story about a little girl who had spiritual insight beyond her years. She was a Christian and perhaps one of those "angelic" believers God places here and there throughout the world. After reading the story of the Lord Jesus' death on the cross for the sins of everyone, including her own, the little girl said to her mother, "Mommy, isn't that just like God?" With her child-faith, she saw through the tragedy of the cross—the ultimate of man's depravity—to the ultimate expression of love coming from the very heart of God. This is what everyone should see in the cross of Calvary: the worst man can do answered by the sacrificial love of God.

In everything, good and bad, our heavenly Father moves in grace and mercy to enhance or override the efforts of us weak, misguided human beings. When we attempt to do something good, He intervenes to beautify our endeavors to make them even more attractive and appealing and beneficial. In the same way, when we commit some terrible atrocity, He intercedes to bring something propitious and significant out of the rubble. For example, some years ago when movie stars and other celebrities gathered to record the song, "We Are the World," and to donate all the proceeds to needy causes, the question was asked, "Where are the Christians? Why didn't they do something? They're always preachin' love and God and all that stuff. Where are they?" The answer was simple:

Believers have been doing "something" all along. The Christians have led the way from the beginning. Missionaries and Christian organizations have been "out there" doing something since Christianity began. The good that "We Are the World" generated brought this out, and more people were helped and exposed to the message of the Gospel.

On the other side, when terrorists struck on September 11, 2001, the shock sent Americans reeling, and the perpetrators thought that they had destroyed our sense of security and freedom. Yes, a lot of people were rattled and didn't know where to turn. But it did not take long for the American people to catch their balance and regroup. Leading the way was our President, George W. Bush, himself a Christian, Dr. Billy Graham, and other well-known Christians who gave everyone hope, a sense of pride, and a commitment to God and country. Thousands of Christian ministers across the nation brought their congregations together in love and in a rededication to the Lord. Many believers saw a new urgency to share their faith in Jesus Christ with family, friends, and neighbors. No, we Christians did not handle the opportunity perfectly. We never do. And there were some negative aspects to the tragedy as there always is where human beings are involved. But God took this evil act and brought many dear souls into a saving relationship with His Son, and that is the most important result in the travesty. And…isn't that just like God?

We should see the hand of our loving God in everything. He is not detached or far removed from His creation, especially us human beings. Whether we achieve something good or commit a heinous deed, He comes to add His divine touches to the good and to rescue us from the destruction of the evil. He helps at all times and in all ways. He even moves in the life of a little cat.

Tiffany, the unassuming, mild-mannered feline part of the Shaffer household, is a small "angelic" kitty who was strategically placed by God, I am convinced, in our home at the right time. While Taffy can be "angel-like" at times, she is not a "cherubic" cat such as Tiffy. Now I am not claiming that our little gray and white furball is a real angel incarnate in kittycat flesh. I am not saying that God could not or would not send one of His heavenly beings in feline or any form He so desires. But I am saying that our Father above does create and dispatch certain people and animals into the life and times of individuals here on earth. Brenda and I believe this has happened to us with our parishioners and, of course, Taffy and Tiffany.

In regard to Tiffers, we see in her a kind of female Barnabas. His name means, "Son of encouragement," and Barnabas lived up to his name. See Acts 4:36,37; 11:22-26; 15:36-41. Tiff just oozes love and goodness, and sometimes we think that her little heart is going to burst with all the love it contains. She wants to be with us most of the time, or at least near us, being the purrrfect companion. When we are discouraged or feeling down, our little "encourager" lifts our spirits with her soothing presence and comforting meows. The Apostle Paul tells us to do likewise:

> *So then, invest yourselves, as the chosen ones of God, as holy people, and as those who have been dearly loved, with tender feelings of compassion, kindness, a lowliness of mind, a consideration of others, an enduring patience* (Colossians 3:12).

"Kitty Kare?" Care coming from a cat? Love, unconditional and real? You bet! We encourage everyone to experience a pet, preferably a cat. It can be a journey of joy and love and peace, an adventure worth the effort. Isn't that just like God?

CHAPTER 4

HEARTBREAKING NEWS

In May, I noticed that Taffy seemed to be having some trouble urinating in the litter box. Of course this meant our little Miss Kitty was going to the animal hospital for a check-up. As I stated before, our two furry pals are family to Brenda and I, and so we take good care of them. We made an appointment with Dr. Salzmann, and after examining Taff, he decided to admit her. She was bound up a little and was passing some blood. It was not unusual for Taff to be bound up and to have trouble discharging her stools. The urinary problem was not terribly unusual either and seemed to indicate an infection of some kind. We learned that urinary infections are more common in male cats.

It was difficult leaving Taffy but we knew it was necessary and that she was in good hands. May 5th was our nineteenth wedding anniversary, and although we went out for dinner, we had to struggle to concentrate on the occasion. For some reason everything seems to happen to Taffy, and like loving, concerned parents with a child, we were a little worried. Of course, we pray for our kitties and we prayed for the Tassy. It is best to put everyone and everything in God's hands.

Sunday through Tuesday of that week, we called the animal hospital (Brenda mostly did the calling) to see how the little patient was doing. The staff always gave us an up-to-date report on our little Snookers, as we called her. One of the staff members told Brenda that we could come to visit with her and this made us happy and a bit relieved. I was downtown at the time and when I got home, my wife called me from the hospital.

"Would you like to see Taffy?" she asked encouragingly.

"I'll be right there!" I answered, and took off for the hospital.

When I arrived, Brenda was sitting on a long bench outside one of the exam rooms holding the Taffers who was stretched out on her tummy. She was frightened somewhat because of where she was and the presence of other people in the waiting room, but I knew that she was very happy to see us. Brenda had taken her brush and a couple of toys into the hospital earlier in the week, and the staff told us that she loved to be brushed. When I came in, Brenda had the brush and was grooming our little girl, and I'm sure it made her more content. We spent about 45 minutes or so with Taffy, and it hurt to have to leave her, especially when she cried as the tech took her away.

FINICKY AND FASTIDIOUS

At first, Taffy wouldn't eat for them at the hospital, not even her high-fiber diet food. They monitored her around the clock, watching her litter box habits, food and water intake. During the day, she was content to sleep and was quite unresponsive, but during the night she was more alert and sociable. Not unusual since cats can be nocturnal creatures. Finally, after experimenting with different types of cat food, they resorted to baby food—hand-fed, of course. She would eat this off their fingers, and it was a relief to see her finally ingest some kind of nourishment. Taffy likes to be catered to and allowed Brenda to hand-feed her after surgery years ago. Everyone, I think, likes to be pampered a bit. She finally did start to eat some of her regular food which made us all happy.

When we spoke with Dr. Salzmann, he informed us that our kitty was a "fastidious groomer." We knew that Taffy was a very particular pussycat in everything she did, but Dr. Salzmann told us that she took great efforts to wash and clean herself, more so than most cats. Of course this meant that we should brush Taffy more often because of the loose hair. Little Miss Multi-Colored is a domestic short-hair, but her hair is longer than Tiffany's and she is more susceptible to furballs. The fact that she cleans herself so often and for long periods of time, raises the amount of fur she ingests during her grooming sessions. So Brenda and I determined that we would brush her more often, and of course, she was delighted.

I often said that Taffy's medical records looked like a criminal's rap sheet. They became more so! Her week-long stay at the animal hospital added more pages to her records as she received treatment for her condition. Tassy was discharged on Friday, May 11th with instructions to Brenda and I and an appointment for a return visit. At this point, her urine problem had improved but we were to watch her. We took her in for a follow-up visit on May 23rd and then in July with Tiffany for their yearly check-up and the usual inoculations. Things seemed to be going fairly well and both kitties received good reports.

MORE PROBLEMS

In August, we noticed Taffy having more trouble in the litter box and so we took her to the animal hospital once again. She was examined by Dr. Beverly Shaw who suggested keeping her overnight to check her urine and observe her toilet habits. Again, there was an infection in her urine with evidence of some infection in the kidneys. Dr. Shaw informed us that a long-term antibiotic treatment may be in store. Of course, the Kitty just loved having us administer the drops and kept a wary eye on us at all times. Dr. Shaw prescribed a recheck on Taffy's urine after three weeks.

We actually took her in before that because we were concerned with the problems she was having and seemed to be getting worse. On August 30th, Dr. Case examined Taffy, and along with Dr. Shaw, recommended a series of injections to help calm our high-strung kitty. Like humans, trauma and stress can affect the physiological functions in a cat. Dr. Case set up a schedule for us, and about every three days we took Taffy in for her shot. In all, she received about eleven injections, and the technicians always remarked about how good a cat she was. Of course, we felt that way, but we are a little biased.

We continued the injections through September and into mid-October. Taffy seemed more serene but her urine troubles did not improve. I began to have some real fears about the condition of our little furry friend. On October 9th, two anxious parents took their beloved feline to the animal hospital for an emergency check-up. The veterinarian on duty was Dr. Beverly Shaw who examined Taffy and took an x-ray to try to find any problems. The x-ray was inconclusive and we discussed further options and possibilities with Dr. Shaw after talking about the more invasive procedures available to us, we decided that exploratory surgery was the best way to go. Dr. Shaw would confer with Dr. Salzmann and the other vets to see if this was their feeling as well.

SURGERY IS THE CHOICE

Dr. Salzmann and the staff agreed that surgery was the best option and Monday, October 22nd, was the day selected. We took Taffy in that morning with hopes and prayers that everything would be all right. Dr. Salzmann performed the exploratory surgery and found an inoperable tumor 3/4 the size of her bladder. It was on the back side of the bladder where an x-ray or an ultra-sound would not reveal it.

A technician called around 10:15 that morning to inform us of the situation. I had just returned from doing my banking and Brenda met me at the back door. With tears in her eyes, she related the story to me and said that the technician suggested euthanasia. I responded quickly: "No! I want to talk to Dr. Salzmann first and I have to see Taffy!" Brenda agreed, of course, and we called to ask if Dr. Salzmann could call us when he had time.

It wasn't long before Dr. Salzmann called us and explained the results of the surgery. He told us to keep her as quiet as possible when she came home, and to give her anything she wanted. He said that the tumor was very aggressive and would continue to grow, and that we should watch her to make sure she was urinating. When she could no longer urinate…we knew what had to be done at that point, but we didn't want to hear it.

That evening I was on my way to make a visit, and I stopped by the animal hospital to drop off a photo they loaned us of the tumor, showing how large it was, and, in my opinion, how ugly! While I was at the desk talking with the receptionist, Dr. Salzmann saw me and called me back to one of the exam rooms to explain some more about Taffy's situation. He said that the tumor no doubt had been there a long time. No x-ray or ultra-sound, or any test, would have revealed the tumor in its location.

Toward the end of our conversation, Dr. Salzmann advised, "Don't let her suffer—she's too good of a cat!" I assured him that we would not do that because we loved her too much. I said no matter what happened, Taffy would be remembered for a long time. Our good doctor friend said, "She will live on in her book."

TAFFY COMES HOME

The next day, we picked up Taffers at the animal hospital. Although a bit groggy, our kitty was glad to see us and squirmed to come to us. Brenda noticed an IV needle in her left front leg and called it to the attention of the technician. When the tech tried to take her from Brenda, she received some stiff resistance. After the tech brought her back, Taff was very happy to get into her pet taxi because she knew that she was going home. Our little patient seemed so content when we opened her pet taxi and tried to inspect her surroundings although not being too sure on her feet. Brenda decided to stay close to her and keep an eye on her the rest of the day.

We sat on the bed discussing the situation, still pretty much stunned at this turn of events. I said to my wife, "I feel numb."

She agreed, and added, "It's just so unbelievable. Why Taffy?" I said the same thing to myself, and by the question we did not mean, "Why not Tiffany or someone else's cat?" We just meant why our Taffy? We were hoping to have her as our little baby for many more years. Like most people who receive bad news, we went through the familiar stages of denial, mourning, anger, and questioning God. Of course, as a pastor and wife, we knew better, but "The flesh is weak" (Matthew 26:41).

And like many people with a terminal loved one, I tried to pull out all the stops. In my conversation with Dr. Salzmann, I asked him about a "bladder transplant" or an "artificial bladder." He explained that although veterinary medicine had come a long way, it had not advanced that far. Even though the tumor was localized in the bladder and had not spread, there was not much that could be done at this point. Dr. Salzmann said that if Taffy was an outdoor cat, he could remove the bladder, tumor and all, and run the ureter tubes from the kidneys right to the urethra. However, with this arrangement Taff would have not control of her urine and we could not have this in the house. With an outdoor cat the situation would not be as bad. If there was any way to do something for our kitty, we would have done it.

That afternoon I made a couple of professional visits, but Brenda stayed close to Taffy and watched her every move. She made us flinch when she jumped up on the bed or the toy box, both of which are quite high, but we knew we could not really stop her from jumping. It just caused us undue apprehension to see her do things we thought she shouldn't be doing. At bedtime, I decided to sleep in the spare bedroom and let Taffy sleep with Mommy so she would have enough room to stretch out.

The next morning our little girl gave us quite a scare. In their nearly 15 years of life, these two kitties have had a minimal amount of accidents outside the littler box. Something has to be drastically wrong to cause them to be remiss in their toilet habits. We are quite proud of our "kiddies" in this regard as well as other areas of their feline lives. This morning, however, we were concerned less with our kitty's faithful adherence to the litter box.

DID SHE KNOW?

I heard Brenda cry out from our bedroom and knew that something was wrong. I ran over as fast as I could and she pointed to the clothes basket containing sheets and pillowcases. They were covered with blood, a lot of blood! We recoiled with fear when we saw it laying in puddles in the bottom of the basket. Immediately we located Taffy who seemed to be all right, but the loss of that amount of blood concerned us.

I quickly called the animal hospital and spoke with one of the vets who said that such a discharge of blood was not abnormal in Taffy's condition. If she continued to pass large amounts of blood we were to bring her over. We kept a watchful eye on her and the problem did not reoccur. Every once in a while we did see some blood in her little spots of urine in the litter box. This too, we understood was normal with such a malignant tumor.

But why did Taffy jump in the clothes basket? Did she sense that this issue of blood was coming, or that something was wrong at least? In any event, the little darling refused to do anything on the floor, and we were touched by her consideration. Our two kitties have been accidentally shut in a closet or downstairs, and when they were discovered, ran to the litter box. They did not do their business outside the box. Now, this did not happen often because Brenda and I have always made it our business to know their whereabouts, especially when we went away.

I have heard many pet lovers say that these creatures of God know more than we are aware of. Veterinarians and animal researchers have echoed the same sentiment. No, they are not on a par with humans, but it often seems that they are. When it comes to love, loyalty, understanding, and dedication, many times they outshine us to our shame! Again, we can learn from the animals.

We quickly found Taffy and consoled her and checked her to see if she was in any pain or discomfort. The Taffers will tell us if she has a problem. She usually jumps up on the bed and lies down flat on her side and meows pathetically. If we touch or pet her, this "different" meow becomes more intensified and pitiful. When she goes through this routine or walks around crying for no other reason than being a cat, we know that something is wrong.

After giving our kitty some affection and reassurance, Brenda washed the sheets and pillowcases and they were like new. We have two laundry baskets and we decided to leave them out—one in our bedroom and the other in the spare bedroom—for Taffy's convenience. Brenda put some old sweat outfits in them to absorb any urine or blood, and we did find her utilizing the baskets from time to time.

Once more, my life-partner and I looked at each other, amazed and a little dazed at our wonderful feline friend. The blood problem did not happen again and only infrequently did we find any dampness in the clothes baskets or other places she slept. Although Taffy is her "own cat" so to speak, there is a lot of love bound up in her little heart, and we know that we have a special kitty in our care. I am sure that she knows we love her with all our hearts, and she expects to be doted over. We are just happy to do the doting.

When we took her to the animal hospital to have her stitches out, Dr. Jacklyn Rapp was the attending physician and she took Taffy in another room to remove the sutures. Upon returning to the exam room, Dr. Rapp said to us, "You have a very popular Kitty. As I took her back everyone said, 'Hey, there's Taffy,' and they all made a fuss over her." We explained that she had been coming in at least twice a week for shots so the techs got a chance to know her. "Well, Dr. Rapp replied, "They really like her!" Brenda and I were not surprised. Animal lovers recognize special cats and dogs, and other pets, and can see the unique traits in their personalities. We felt blessed to have been given the privilege of being owned by this extremely nice pussycat. We didn't know what the future held for Taffy, but we realized that God knew that this was going to happen and He would get us through. We decided right away to commit our Kitty and this whole situation to Him.

CONVALESCENT KITTY

Taffy used her litter box quite often, leaving little spots of urine and from time to time we saw some blood in the clumps of litter. We cleaned them out as soon as possible. She slept a lot following the surgery but still insisted on jumping up on the bed and other high places. We could only stand by helplessly and watch.

Brenda stayed close to the house in order to be near Taffy and observe her in case something happened. Half-heartedly we kidded about our "convalescent kitty" and that we were "cat caregivers," but our hearts were really breaking. We prayed and cried a lot as we thought about the possibility of giving up our precious baby girl. It's something no pet owner wants to think about but knows is an inevitable reality. Animals get sick and die just like we do. It is something we all must face.

Brenda again kept the home fires burning, spending a lot of time with Taffy and observing her with the litter box. Our main concern was that she was still passing her urine. She seemed a little more perky and even a bit playful. I did some afternoon visiting and then came home to spend time with the Taffers.

That evening we had a Pastor's Appreciation Banquet to attend at the Edison Hotel in town. The dinner is sponsored by the Gideons International in honor of local ministers whose churches support this missionary organization. If you are not familiar with the Gideons, they are a world-wide group of Christian businessmen who place Bibles in hotels, doctor's offices, hospitals, businesses, and anywhere they are invited to distribute God's Word. They also hand out pocket New Testaments on prep-school and college campuses where they are allowed. These dedicated Christian men also witness for the Lord as they distribute Bibles and have been very successful in winning young and old to the Savior. It is a ministry worth supporting.

The folks at the Edison Hotel are always so accommodating and that evening, Kathy Raker, one of our St. Elias members, was on duty as hostess. Kathy and her daughter and son, Lindsay and Ryan, are animal lovers and were very sympathetic to our situation with Taffy. Kathy, herself, has had enough physical problems to fill a book but doesn't complain and is a dedicated Christian, wife, and mother. We call her our "little trooper." I feel blessed to have her as a sister-in-the-Lord and as a member of our church.

The banquet began at 6:00 p.m. and Brenda left shortly after the meal to be with Taffy. I explained the situation to some of our hosts among the Gideons, and these wonderful people were completely understanding. We sat with good friend Bob Reich and his wife, Virginia, and we shared concerns with them about Taffy. Bob is the Lay Pastor at Mountain Presbyterian Church, not far from our two churches, and is the leader of a men's prayer group that meets every Friday morning at 6:00 a.m. I am also a member of the group, and we meet in a different area church each month. We have about twelve faithful men who gather to pray for the pastors and congregations in the county and, really, around the world. We pray for our nation, for Israel, and for all the people on this troubled earth. We have seen tremendous answers to prayer, and we cherish our fellowship and time together.

During our conversation with Bob and Virginia, I asked Bob

how he felt about me bringing up Taffy as a prayer request the next morning. He said that he saw nothing wrong with praying for a pet since they are God's creatures. We agreed that we have a great group of guys who are understanding and loving. Brenda and I felt better with good prayer warriors holding our kitty up before her God. We knew that He loved her as He does all His wonderful critters. We had peace about Taffy no matter the outcome.

The next morning, I went to the prayer meeting and asked the men if they would keep Taffy in their prayers. No one snickered at the thought of praying for a cat, but everyone offered comfort and empathy to Brenda and I because they knew how we treasured her. I told them that if they had a problem praying for an animal just to pray for my wife and I. Not one expressed such a concern, but offered up petitions for Taffy and us. One of our men, Tom Gresh, recalled an incident in his church when one of the children's pets, a gerbil, I think, was missing and someone told the pastor. Everyone sympathized with the distraught youngster and the whole church prayed that the gerbil would be found. I revel that Christian people respond so lovingly when a member of God's family is hurting, even when it involves a pet.

After prayer meeting and some coffee time at Jay's Restaurant, I returned home to do some work in my study and to watch over the Taffers. Brenda had left shortly before I got home to work for one of our members and had left a note telling me what she had done with the kitty. Periodically I checked on her as she spent time in their kitty house, her pillow under the crib, and the bed. After Brenda came home, we also began taking a lot of pictures and giving her a lot of attention. We thought sometimes that Taff sensed that she had a serious problem because she craved our attention and company.

Brenda stayed with her while I attended a funeral in the afternoon and then when I did some necessary work in the garage. It wasn't too cold so I kept the door open and noticed Taffy watching me from the spare bedroom window. I moved my project outside so that she could see me and the little mowlskers watched me the entire time. Of course, I hurried a bit so that I could get back down to her and give her my undivided attention, as much as that was possible. Upon going upstairs, Brenda and I got a surprise as we entered our bedroom. Lying on the bed was the notorious purple ball, "planted" by you-know-who while I was up at the garage and when Brenda had gone downstairs for a moment. As soon as we entered the room, a well-known calico kitty appeared and hopped up on the bed ready to play. With tears in our eyes, we accommodated her, cautiously, due to her surgery just five days before. As I recall, my wife managed to say quietly, "What a melt-the-heart pussycat!" I nodded in total agreement.

ACCEPTING THE UNACCEPTABLE

Some years ago a TV commercial for a manufacturer's product depicted a housewife refusing to substitute an inferior brand for their merchandise. When an unseen sponsor offered her the "other" product, she blurted out, "No! That is totally unacceptable to me!" As I watched the ad, I thought how pretentious it sounded. "People don't normally respond that way," I reasoned. But this was a TV commercial and the sponsors were trying to impress the public and influence people to buy their product. Often they are more successful than we realize.

As I pondered our situation with Taffy, I came to the conclusion that we Christians react with the same response to the adversities of life all too often: "That is unacceptable to me!" And, in all honesty and in reality, it is directed toward God whom we feel could have and should have prevented this bad thing from happening to us. After all, aren't we His favorites? I used to laugh when Fonzie said this on *Happy Days,* looking up to heaven, "And I thought I was Your favorite!" However, our spiritual relationship with God is no laughing matter. We need to rise above the petty reasoning and reactions of the old nature, and act like the dignified and honorable people we are called by the Lord to be. The Apostle James stated it in a straight forward, matter-of-fact way.

Who is wise and has expertise among you? Let him demonstrate, by a noble response to the adversity of life, his positive actions in an attitude of humility, which is prompted by love (James 3:13)

The world is watching! Watching Christians to see how they respond to tragedy, sorrow, outrage, bad news, and all the negative experiences of life. Some are observing to find reasons to criticize and find fault. Some are watching out of curiosity and others are looking for answers and hope! Our responsibility as believers is to respond nobly and set an alluring and life-changing example. How do we know the number of people we may win over to God's side? The important and vital issue is how we handle ourselves in such situations.

The news about Taffy was devastating to Brenda and I, but I feel that we responded in a manner becoming of Christians. Sure, we cried and are still crying, and no doubt always will when we think of it because we love her so much. It was "unacceptable" to us, this cruel, intangible enemy called cancer that invaded our territory and threatened to take away our beloved kitty. However, we had to accept the cold, hard fact of the situation and adjust our lives accordingly.

It is in times like this when our faith in the Lord is our greatest ally. He knows personally what it is to experience the sad, sorrowful, traumatic occurrences of life. In His Son, Jesus Christ, He has felt the pang and pain in every human heart. He knows better than anyone else what it is to watch someone you love suffer and not really be able to do anything about it. "He...gave Him up for us all," the Apostle Paul tells us in Romans 8:32 to a cold, heartless mob who nailed Him to a cross! So He knows! And He cares!

Praise be given to the God and Father of our Lord Jesus Christ, the Father of Compassion and the God of all comfort, who comforts us in all our distresses (2 Corinthians 1:3-4).

Brenda and I decided to commit Taffy to the Lord and trust in Him no matter what the future held. In this we took comfort, that our loving, heavenly Father would be at our side through it all, and that He would be with Taffy, too. That's the kind of Father He is. Praise be to God!

CHAPTER FIVE

SOME WONDERFUL PEOPLE

I t has been my privilege and pleasure to mingle my life with the lives of some very unique and marvelous people during my tenure on God's green earth. I haven't met many celebrities in this time—Dr. Tim LaHaye, Dr. John Wesley White, and Franklin Graham to name a few—but I count the folks I have encountered as notable as anyone, and especially esteemed in the sight of the Lord. When all is said and done and the final tally is in, I have an idea that the real "celebs" will be those who were unknown as far as the world's estimate is concerned, but of great notoriety in the heavenly realms. The final result is the important one—the one that will last for eternity.

In God's eyes the important one is the missionary laboring in some dark corner of the world; the housewife making her home a spiritual and loving refuge for her family; the secretary or receptionist making her boss look good and spreading cheer and hope to those she meets; the factory worker who sets a good example in attitude and toil; the teacher who tries to influence the students for God despite the limitations imposed upon him/her; the waitress who offers words of encouragement to her customers while filling up their coffee cups; the businessman who sees his client's real needs as well as what they wish to transact with his company; the doctor who treats the whole patient whether he has insurance or not; the lawyer who uses the law to help people, not to fill his pockets; and many, many more.

Of course, the folks I am talking about are Christians who see their professions as a channel through which to share the Gospel of the Lord Jesus Christ. Whether in word or deed or both, they share His love and compassion with others, hoping to bring them into a saving relationship with Him. They are not antagonistic, arrogant, or abrasive. They do not attempt to jam the Gospel down anyone's throat. They live their faith in an inviting and charming way so that people are not offended and driven away from the Savior. They love people and see them as potential believers—candidates for the family of God. They don't take people as they are, they take them for what He can make them. They see through the veneer of human nature to the image of God, which, although somewhat obscured, is still there. I see them as the mighty power of God, lovingly and quietly making a difference in the world without any pomp and fanfare. This is the way it should be, for they are not out to draw attention to themselves, but to draw attention to the Lord Jesus. To glorify the Savior, to decrease while He increases (John 3:30) is what it means to be a Christian.

Most of the profound people I have met in my lifetime were Christians, and they have had a positive influence in my life. I have had the fortune to meet many nice folks over the years, not all of them of the Christian faith, but wonderful individuals because God created them. I only pray and hope that I exerted a favorable influence upon them which might be used by the Holy Spirit to attract them to the Lord Jesus. Our efforts are always imperfect, so we need the help of God in living for Him and in serving Him. May He bolster our feeble attempts to add to His Kingdom. I now wish to introduce you to some admirable people who touched our lives, especially in the ordeal we were about to face with Taffy.

THE BELOVED VETERINARIAN

As I have mentioned in Cats I and previously in this book, we cannot express enough our appreciation for Dr. George Salzmann, our kitties' physician. For two decades he has cared for our pets and we are grateful for his kindness and genuine concern. As Taffy would tell you, this "Doc" has a nice bedside manner. Most animals are quite apprehensive when taken to the vet and their "people" try to calm their fears as best they can. After arriving at the animal hospital, the staff and especially the veterinarian can do much to assuage their fright. Dr. Salzmann has this sincere love for animals, and I am convinced, a gift from God in working with and treating the Lord's many fascinating critters. Brenda and I are amazed at how he can quiet Taff and Tiff and get them to realize that he means them no harm. Now, they do not get super upset and rowdy, but we can tell that they are afraid. With his understanding and knowledge of animals and his devotion to them, their pet doctor makes our kiddies feel better.

Dr. Salzmann also makes us feel better. He explains things to us—and other pet owners—so that we know exactly what is going on. He makes you feel comfortable and at ease about your pet's health and condition. If he uses medical terms that we are not familiar with, he always interprets them for us. Since he is such an intelligent man, sometimes we have to ask him to "interpret" the interpretation. Without a tinge of impatience he carefully defines the situation, often drawing a picture to help us comprehend the circumstances more fully. Like a good practitioner, he is thorough and lets no stone unturned. When I mention his name to fellow pet lovers, they express the highest regard for and confidence in this fine gentleman. Dr. Salzmann and his wife, Ann, are loving parents dedicated to their family, who are scattered across the country, and to their "pet family" which consists of cats and dogs and other furry pals.

This beloved "Sunbury Sawbones" often goes above and beyond the call of duty for his clients. Two of my parishioners, Bob and Betty Jane Renn, members of our Zion Church, are animal lovers and have had dogs and cats over the years. Bob is more of a canine person and Betty Jane is feline inclined, but they enjoy the company of furry friends. You may recall from Cats I that Bob is quite a jokester and loves to tease Betty Jane and Brenda about caring for their kitties. And you may recall how one of their beloved puppies saved Bob's life during a seizure. Their pets are very dear to them.

When we came to the churches in 1984, Bob and Betty Jane

had a sheep dog named Pepper. She was not a young dog then and the time came when her health failed and they had to have her put to sleep. Pepper was big and could not get around too well, and the thought of taking her to the vet was too traumatic. Even their son, Roger, was reluctant to make the fateful trip. They consulted with Dr. Salzmann who volunteered to come to their home and perform the deed of mercy.

After a while Bob and Betty Jane got another dog, a Golden Retriever, whom they name Lacy. It was Lacy who responded to save Bob's life and, of course, this endeared her to Bob. The years passed and the time came again for this nice couple to face the dreaded decision. Dr. Salzmann came to the rescue once more and traveled to their home to help ease the pain of the situation. I know that Bob and Betty Jane truly appreciated the kindness and consideration. When Brenda and I adopted Taff and Tiff, Betty Jane and Bob recommended Dr. Salzmann. We could see why right away. He has that genuine love and concern for the pets and their people who become his clients. He has their best interests at heart and makes both parties feel at ease with his reserved and quiet demeanor. In my opinion, he is a cut above and has fulfilled his calling from God whether he practices another day or not. Thank you, good doctor!

A KITTY KARD FROM A KINDHEARTED KOUPLE

When I announced Taffy's condition to the people in our churches and requested their prayers, we received sympathies and promises of prayer from nearly everyone. It is just an evidence of the close relationship that we have with our wonderful folks at Zion and St. Elias. These two churches—or congregations—are "families" in the true sense of the word. Brenda and I know that we are blessed to be their pastor and wife, and we thank God for them.

One Sunday after my announcement about Taffy, a family I mentioned in Chapter one—Grant, Holly, and Casey Renninger—presented us with a greeting card as they were leaving the service. We had no inkling at the time just why Grant and Holly gave us the card or what the occasion might be. This is nothing unusual, however, as our people will send us cards spontaneously for no other reason than to say thank you or offer encouragement. One of our ladies at St. Elias, Shirley Kemberling, is very sagacious in this area and has excellent taste in greeting cards, sensing which card will fit the need. Believe me—it helps!

Holly has this ability, too, and the card she handed us that Sunday was a large one, featuring a "Maine Coon" on the cover. The cat looks something like an Angora with long hair, but the card gives an explanation inside that the Maine Coon is America's oldest long-haired cat breed. It comes in many colors from white to tortoiseshell. Neither Brenda nor I ever heard of this breed of cat, but I later learned that a friend of ours, Laura Long, a waitress at Jay's (my favorite coffee haunt), had a Maine Coon sometime ago. Laura saw the card one morning at the restaurant as I was doing some writing on this chapter, and remarked that it looked a lot like her cat. She is one of the over sixty million cat lovers in this country with the numbers continuing to grow.

What most touched Brenda and I was what Holly wrote in the card. I want to share this very kind thought with you. It is an example of the love we have been shown by our terrific people.

Dear Clair and Brenda,

We hope that Taffy will make it through many more wonderful years with you. She is very lucky to have "parents" like the two of you!

Love,

Grant, Holly and Casey

If I remember correctly, we called and thanked Holly for the touching words and the nice card after lunch that Sunday. It would be a keepsake and placed with the kitties' records in their file for now. Isn't it wonderful to have such considerate and gracious friends in Christ Jesus our Lord? We treasure them all! And if anyone was wondering—yes—the card was a Hallmark!

THE LADY WITH A MENAGERIE

A few years ago, Judy Ressler began coming to St. Elias with her grandson, Jeremy. Judy, and husband, Ron, bought the property that previously belonged to Pete and Clara Boone after a fire devastated their home. Pete had built an addition to their split-level and had constructed a huge, beautiful fireplace that filled the room. He put this room together with the best top-grade material and heavy lumber. The split-level was poorly constructed and assembled with inferior materials. It went up in smoke like a tinder box. Pete's addition was barely singed. Like a Christian's work through the Holy Spirit, it had stood the test.

Judy and Ron inspected the room and fell in love with it right away. With a few repairs and clean-up, it would be as good as new. They added a beautiful A-frame type home adjoined to the surviving room. The two compliment each other. It was a good job, and the Resslers are enjoying it immensely.

Now this family are animals lovers and have a wide variety of God's creatures. I understand that the main culprit here is Judy who is a "softie" for critters who need a home and some TLC. Among this menagerie are dogs—including a St. Bernard—cats, a bird, and a donkey. Brenda and I met some of them and must say they certainly are pampered pets.

Judy also has a big heart for people and maybe animal lovers in particular. She is employed by a retail chain store and loves to help her customers. She is a great asset to her employer, and as a Christian she is a benefit also to the Kingdom of the Lord Jesus Christ. At church when I made the announcement about Taffy having cancer, Judy offered sympathy, understanding, and helpful information. Over the next couple of weeks, Judy talked with us over the phone to offer more encouragement and good suggestions. During that same time, I went to the store where she works and spoke with her at her station. While discussing Taffy's condition, I broke down a bit and Judy gave me a much needed hug. I left the store feeling better because of a caring and understanding sister-in-the-Lord. Judy's help and reassurances to us are greatly appreciated.

THE DUKE'S ROYAL PAIR

Harry and Anna Moyer have been friends of ours for nearly as long as we have been with the churches. I just wrote about Pete Boone earlier in the book and in this chapter. Well, Anna is Pete's sister and she and Harry live beside the Resslers where Pete and Clara used to live before the fire. A few years ago, Harry and Anna transferred their membership to St. Elias and immediately became active workers for the Lord. If someone asks for help at the church or the parsonage, Harry is right there to lend a hand. Anna has some severe physical disabilities, but is a great cook and baker and always makes sure that there is enough food and goodies at the church when we have a fellowship dinner. Of course, Brenda, Mary and I are the happy recipients of Anna's luscious fudge and baked goods at Christmas time and other occasions. Needless to say, we are glad that Harry and Anna are on board at the I.H.S. St. Elias Ship (I.H.S. meaning "In His Service").

You may have wondered about the paragraph heading, The Duke's Royal Pair." Well, the Duke is Harry and Anna's Springer Spanier, a white puppy spotted with dark brown patches, and full of vim and vigor. Harry and Anna are Duke's Royal Pair—they are royalty to him and his special people. Now of course, Duke is very special to Harry and Anna, too. He is their pride and joy, and they love to spoil him with toys and treats. Duke has the run of the house and sleeps or naps where he darn well pleases, and at night plops in with Harry and Anna. And, as they will tell you, he takes his half outa' the middle. Harry might tell you that sometimes Duke can be a "royal pain," but they put up with it because they love him.

Harry and Anna are "royal" to us, too, being loving and sympathetic friends and Christians who have had the experience of an ill pet. They do not have a cat at this time, but they have had some feline friends in the past who meant a lot to them. Just some years ago they had a kitty who had procured a big space in their hearts, and when the time came to end the suffering, it was difficult and traumatic. At church, at church functions, and while visiting them, Harry and Anna have consoled us, encouraged us, and offered to help in any way. They have been a great blessing to us. They know the score and they understand because they've been there.

AN "ODD COUPLE?"

As we entered Gale and Jodie's house, Brenda and I were greeted by Zeus, a beautiful Great Dane puppy. Zeus was the "big" surprise and he was a big baby. Brenda was the first to give him a hug and make a fuss over him, having had a Dane some years before. Zeus reminded me of my Boxer dog, Rinny, albeit in a larger version.

As we all settled in for a visit, Zeus joined right in, vying for our attention but at the same time being quite the gentleman. I watched my wife petting and talking to our canine counterpart, knowing that this meeting was arousing a few memories, some good and some bad. She, of course, had to share her experiences with Jodie and Gale as the evening drew on, and at times, I thought I could detect a quiver in her voice as she related some not-so-pleasant incidents with her Dane. Her older brother, Jim, at one time raised these magnificent animals and Brenda had her share of heartbreaking circumstances when things did not go right and some errors were made in diagnosis by the vet. Yet, she did have many happy memories of loving and caring for her huge friend. She even had thoughts of going on to school to become a veterinarian because of her love for dogs

That desire did not materialize but Brenda is still fascinated by veterinary medicine and interrogates our vets when the Kitties go to the animal hospital. She is not content to just go through the dispensing of medication or this or that procedure, she wants to know the what and why of the instructions. Our vets accommodate her questions but more often than not explain everything so that we know exactly what is being prescribed and why.

As the conversation continued, I retired to a couch located in an adjoining room and was quickly accompanied by Zeus who attempted to sit on my lap. I was taken by surprise and we all laughed as the big puppy tried to adjust himself to my small legs. Brenda has often told me that I "have no lap." However, that did not deter Zeus who adeptly positioned himself on my "non-lap" to everyone's delight.

Jodie informed us that Zeus had claimed the couch as his own and if someone sat on it, this was an invitation for him to sit on their lap. Well, the doggie made no exception in my case and quickly initiated me into his couch fraternity. He made no indication of moving until Jodie and Gale insisted that I was not a good candidate for a comfortable seat. Reluctantly, he conceded and moved over to sit beside me looking somewhat dejected. As I petted him and tried to cheer him up, the other member of this odd couple made her appearance.

Jodie called our attention to the diminutive spy who was peeking at us through the balusters of the stairway near the top. We had to look closely to see what Jodie was talking about and Brenda saw her first—a ferret, whose name was Boo Boo. We quietly expressed our amazement so that we would not frighten her and our tiny new friend made her way down the steps to greet us.

After inspecting us with a careful scrutiny, Boo Boo decided that we were "ferret-safe" and allowed us to pet and hold her. Brenda and I were thrilled by the charm of this little creature who had such a mystical manner of captivating your affection. All of us agreed: God does beautiful and wonderful work.

Boo Boo was very intelligent and seemed to sense that people were quite taken with her. She liked being the center of attention and quickly returned to our gathering after leaving to eat or drink or whatever. She enjoyed the fuss we made over her immensely and her eyes seemed to sparkle with delight.

In the course of our conversation, Jodie and Gale enlightened us about ferrets and their care. We had heard that they were in demand and very popular as pets, but Boo Boo was our first encounter with one up close and personal. It was a good first meeting and we were impressed.

Our hosts informed us that it took a little while for them to catch on to what was happening when some things began to disappear, especially in their bedroom. They actually blamed each other at first, accusing one another of misplacing this or that, or for playing tricks, in a kidding way, of course.

They solved the mystery one day as Jodie was house cleaning and tried to run the sweeper under a chest of drawers in a corner. The attachment would not go back to the wall, and Jodie could feel something, or things, impeding its progress. Upon inspection, she discovered the missing items neatly stacked in the corner and knew immediately that Zeus did not put them there. That left only one suspect and it wasn't Gale. Jodie was happy and relieved to find their things, but couldn't help being amused at the antics of this little bandit.

We laughed as Jodie and Gale related the story to us and said that Boo Boo must be part Pack Rat, but only part because she did not leave anything in return. Jodie explained that they found that this was characteristic of ferrets who accumulate things. Actually the word ferret is from the Latin term *furo*, hence the word "furtive," which means "done by stealth."

Just why ferrets take and hide things is not totally clear, although it has been observed that they hoard all kinds of things from leather key chains to dirty socks. Owners must be on guard as to what they leave lying around.

Brenda and I were further intrigued as Jodie shared yet another aspect of caring for ferrets. It seems that if female ferrets are not bred they will die. Ferret owners who do not wish to mate their pets must take appropriate action to insure the safety of the little gals.

This action includes dispensing birth control pills to the females on a regulated schedule or having them spayed. A female will remain in heat until she is bred or spayed, and even then special care is needed. Brenda spoke to a pet store employee who informed her that all the ferrets they receive are spayed or neutered.

My research for this book revealed that these cute little cuddlies live only six to eight years, although some have reached the ripe age of fourteen. They are very sociable critters, playful, and energetic, which sounds a lot like our two little ones at home. Experts advise owners to spend as much time as they can with their little pals to insure a good relationship and also good health, i.e., well-being.

Our visit with Jodie and Gale was a very pleasant and rewarding one as they were gracious hosts, and, of course, we thoroughly enjoyed Zeus and Boo Boo. We marveled at how they got along and how the big puppy carefully placed his huge feet so that he would not squash his pint-sized pal. We knew that this unlikely duo would do all right, not just because they adapted to each other and developed a good relationship, but also on account of the love and care they were receiving from Jodie and Gale. They were getting what they needed the most. If all pet owners were only that dedicated and appreciative of their gifts from God!

Gale and Jodie later had children and have raised a wonderful family. The Lord has truly blessed them in many ways and they serve Him faithfully through their Church and other means. They are among the "special people" that God has brought into our lives down through the years and we thank Him for each and every one.

HUGS AND HANDSHAKES

It would take too much space and time to share all the love and concern expressed by the fine folks at St. Elias and Zion. However, I feel compelled to say that our people responded with such compassion to Brenda and I that we were extremely touched. The morning I related Taffy's situation, we received many hugs and handshakes after the service. I would venture to say that nearly every member offered at least a word of encouragement to us. Many said that they would pray for Taffy. A lot of our youngsters and youth said the same. Even some who do not especially care for cats said that they hoped that Taffy would get better. This was for Brenda and I. This was because of their love for us. It is an understatement to say that it meant more to us than words can express.

There was Dale Martz, Gail's husband, who had to have his kitty, Seymour, of nearly 20 years of age, put to sleep. It was almost more than he could bear, but his nephew and next door neighbor, Barry Martz, helped him with the heartbreaking process. Barry is married to Tina, who is Gail's sister—Gail being our St. Elias organist, choir director, and typist of the manuscript for this book. Dale knew exactly what we were going through and sympathized with us in what we might be facing.

Just not long ago, at our Zion Church, Brenda asked Bobbie Long how her Schnauzer, Harley, was doing. Bobbie said, "We had to have him put to sleep yesterday." My wife and I were shocked. We knew that Harley had developed diabetes and we assumed that it became uncontrollable, but Bobbie explained that a blood clot had formed in his spinal cord and caused a paralysis in his one side. There was nothing that could be done; he would not get better. Harley was quite a puppy—loving, friendly, and so intelligent he scared you! He loved carrots, so when we visited with Bob, Ida and Bobbie, Brenda put some small carrots in a plastic bag in her pocket book. Harley always knew right where they were and pestered Brenda until she gave in. You had a tough time fooling him; he knew when you had a treat for him, and Harley was a treat himself.

Although he was Bobbie's dog, Harley was Bob and Ida's buddy, too. He kept them company while his mistress was at work and gave them hours of entertainment. When Ida went home to be with the Lord, Harley was a little lost soul. He didn't know where his Ida went and he missed her dearly. He stuck like glue to Bob while Bobbie was working, so much so that Bob called him his shadow. Maybe he was afraid that Bob would go away, too. They mourn for loved ones as well.

Before Harley came into their lives, Bobbie had a terrier-type puppy named Jake, who wormed his way into the family's heart. We enjoyed visiting with Jake when we came to the Long home, and he did his best to make us feel welcome. It was very difficult for Bobbie when he became ill and had to be put down. So, when Taffy was stricken with cancer, Bobbie and Bob understood how we felt and extended their hearts to us. Isn't this similar to what the Apostle Paul told the Corinthian Christians?

Our heart has been opened wide (2 Corinthians 6:11).

I must share a story about Ida who had a tremendous sense of humor. Everyone kidded her about her punctuality—that is, her lack of it. Of course, the classic wisecrack from family and friends was, "Ida—you're going to be late for your own funeral!" In order to stay true to form and honor Ida's sense of humor, I started her Celebration of Life service at 11:05 a.m.—five minutes late! It was Bobbie's idea, and I think everybody concurred that it was a fitting tribute to a lady who loved life despite all the physical pain she endured most of her short 69 years. We also thought of bringing Harley to the service because of his love for Ida and her affection for him, and Ida's flair for the unusual, but we decided against it out of appreciation for Jerre and David Blank, father and son—who own and operate the funeral home. Jerre and David are very professional and accommodating, but we felt this would be too much to ask. (Of course, we did not seriously consider it, but joked about it as another means to show our love for Ida.) Now Harley would have been the perfect gentleman, but it was out of the question. We all knew that Ida would understand.

One of our St. Elias couples, Jackie and Darlene Semerod, at one time had four Beagles in the house and qualify as top pet lovers in my book. There was Rusty, the patriarch of the group, Daisy, the matriarch, Baby, and Sandy—four! After greeting you with loud barks and an investigation that would make the CIA and the FBI proud, the puppies would settle down and vie for your attention. They got along well and received lots of love from Darlene and Jackie who provided a fine home for their canine companions. When Jackie III came into their lives, we wondered how this would affect the Semerod household—how would the doggies accept this new addition who would require a lot of attention from Mom and Dad. Well, the beagle brigade passed the test and adopted the little guy as part of their family. Animals can adjust to change many times better than we can, and although we are often beset by adjustments, they seem to make the transition more smoothly.

Jackie and Darlene had to make some changes on their part, too, and when Jesse came along a few years later, the process began all over again. As far as the puppies were concerned, they were ready to make some concessions yet another time. Sure, Dad and Mom had to train the boys to be careful around the dogs in some respects because pets have their limitations, but things went well with planning and preparation. This is the secret of raising children and pets together—plan and prepare.

Years pass and take their toll on our furry friends, and this is what happened a few years ago in the Semerod family. While they were on vacation, Baby became ill suddenly and died. She didn't show any signs of being sick when they left, so it was a shock to hear the news. Darlene told me that she cried and cried, feeling guilty because she wasn't there for her puppy in her time of need. Devoted pet lovers are that way. They take it seriously when something happens to their pet whom they consider to be part of their family. Brenda and I offered our sympathies to Darlene and Jackie, not realizing that we would soon being going through a similar experience. When they learned that Taffy was stricken with cancer, they expressed their concerns and hopes for her recovery, and our state of mind. Pet owners are on an exclusive wave-length, able to pick up on each other's feelings or vibes. They can sense and understand how a fellow pet owner is feeling, but with an honest empathy. We appreciated Jackie and Darlene's heartfelt concern and knew that it was real.

I remember when Dick and Norma Willard had a dog named "Charlie," who didn't bark—he just didn't bark! He was so friendly and amicable, and didn't even make a sound if someone stepped on his tail or feet. After he was gone, Dick and Norma chose not to get another pet, and since both retired, they are on the go quite a bit. Now this very nice couple are not cat lovers as such, but Brenda and I got hugs and kisses and promises of prayer because they truly cared. And they kept a check on how Taffy was doing, and Brenda and I, too.

Dot Bailor, who was married to one of the finest men I have ever met, knows what it is to have to give up a beloved pet. Dot, and Harry, who went home to glory eight years ago, had a Lhasa Apso, who was their pride and joy. It hurt them deeply when they had to part with their precious puppy, and Dot still has the photos to help keep his memory alive. She also greatly misses her "buddy," an appropriate designation for Harry who was a joy to be with. He was a fun-loving and devoted Christian who made everyone feel good. So Dot knew what we were going through with Taffy and the bleak prospects we faced, and she could sympathize with us. Dot's daughter, Darlene, had brought along the doggy from overseas so it made this puppy that more special.

Good friends Donald and Ardis Drumm and Martin and Mollie Raker, who have helped Brenda and I more than we could ever hope to repay, had pets at one time and understood our concern. When we came to St. Elias and Zion, we worked closely with these fine people who did much to keep the churches going when some tough times came. We count them among those special people we have had the pleasure to know and love.

Terry and Pam Latsha, Rod and Angie Raker, Gib and Linda Wolfe, Norm and Louise Reitz, their son, Bob and wife, Cheryl, Lyle and Sandy White, Brian and Lottie Kerstetter, Bob and Sheila Radel, Wayne and Linda Renn, Fred and Shirley Moyer, Bill and Gale Brosious, Bruce and Janette Drumm, Peggy Mutschler, Dean Hoover, Fred and Michelle Culp, Evert and Beulah Hoffman, and I am sure others, have or have had dogs and cats. All of these wonderful folks expressed their love and concern for our situation with Taffy. God always provides the right people for the right circumstances. Brenda and I are grateful to Him and them for being there for us in a special way.

I must share another human interest story before closing this chapter about some very wonderful people. I mentioned Evert and Beulah Hoffman above as two of those who understood our pain and did much to ease the ache in our hearts. This very special couple came to St. Elias a few years ago, and as we got to know them better we learned that Evert is not only a World War II veteran, but also a Pearl Harbor survivor. We feel very honored to have such a distinguished serviceman as a friend and member of our church. He is a career Army man with the rank of Major retired, and Lt. Colonel U. S. Army Reserves.

"Moose" as Evert wishes to be called, knew "Boots," as Beulah is known, before the war and wanted to marry her when he came home. The joke goes that Boots had another suitor vying for her hand and he also was in the service overseas, and when they came back she would have to make a choice. Well, we all know who she chose, and I have heard some people say that she made the right one. Well, the Lord was in this match-up and they have been happily married for nearly 60 years. No one that I know of has done more to help people than Moose and Boots. Although they have slowed down a bit, it is still difficult to find them home. They are good will ambassadors on the go to do anything they can to lift the burdens of others.

I was thrilled when Moose asked me to speak at a prayer/breakfast meeting of one of the Pennsylvania chapters of the Pearl Harbor Survivors in a local hotel restaurant a few years ago. I felt honored to meet—and share from God's Word—with these heroes of World war II who fought and survived one of the most treacherous attacks in modern warfare. I had told Moose that I had a soft, warm spot in my heart for WWII veterans because my Dad fought in France and Germany during the War. I respect and am grateful to all our service people. I feel privileged to know Moose and Boots and have them as members of our St. Elias Church. I thank God for them!

"They will be a people blessed" (Isaiah 65:23) as the prophet Isaiah records God's promise to Israel in the Millennial Kingdom, The Jews, who have been hunted, hounded, hated, and hammered for millenniums, look eagerly to the day when the Messiah returns and restores the Kingdom to His chosen people. (Acts 1:6). They look forward to finally living in peace and enjoying the blessings of Jehovah.

Being an Israelite himself, the Apostle Paul knew first hand the meaning of persecution and hardship—both as a Jew and as a Christian. He experienced sorrow and suffering in many ways and was well aware of what it meant to trust in the Lord. He knew, also, how God utilizes other believers to help fellow saints through the tough times by being there, by understanding, by offering a word of comfort—by loving. Paul mentions three such Christian men, Aristarchus, Mark and Justus—three Jewish brothers in the Lord—and says of them, "…they were appointed to be a comfort to me" (Colossians 4:11).

At first glance we might dismiss his comment as a normal description of what people—especially Christians—do for each other and are expected to do for one another. But a closer investigation of the word "comfort" reveals a deeper intention of the great apostle. The Greek word is not the usual term for comfort used in the New Testament, but is the word *paregoria,* from where we get our medical term paregoric. Of course, paregoric is a pain killer—no longer available by prescription or from your doctor—used years ago for various maladies.

This old remedy is a good illustration of what Christians should be to one another: those who help ease the pain of a brother or sister in Jesus Christ. In my translation of the book of Colossians, I translated the word *paregoria* as a "soothing relief." This is a vital ministry or service believers can render to each other, being there as healing instruments in the hands of God. Christians with the spiritual gift of "helps" may be of invaluable use in difficult and traumatic situations. Like no others, they have the supernatural ability to ease the hurt of fellow believers and non-Christians as well.

The people I have mentioned in this chapter and throughout the book, fit the description of paregoria—pain killers indeed! They certainly have eased the ache in Brenda's and my heart. We thank God for them every day, and have realized even more the importance of being a blessing to those around us. The people I have told about will be as Isaiah says, "A people blessed." We all should determine in our hearts to seek to lessen the pain of those we love and even those we don't. That would make the Lord Jesus very happy.

CHAPTER 6

A TRIBUTE TO TAFFY

We continued to monitor Taffy's litter box habits, noting especially her urine output. Yes, it took time but we managed to monitor our kitty and still perform our daily tasks. It's amazing just what you can do if you want to or need to. It is all in the motivation—how much are we dedicated to what we are doing? Brenda and I love Taffy and Tiffy and will do what it takes to help them and keep them safe. They didn't ask to be brought into our home, and we know it is our responsibility to care for them. We have thoroughly enjoyed being "owned" by these two little pudder tats and are grateful to God for sending them into our lives. I feel that we have done well for them, providing a nice environment for them to be their independent "cat selves." We have made many mistakes—especially yours truly—in raising our two feline protégées put in our guardianship by the Lord, but I am confident that our successes far outweigh our failures. Brenda and I do not have any children together, so Taff and Tiff have become our "kids." If you haven't guessed, they are very special to us.

TAFFY COMMITTED TO THE LORD

After a few weeks of resorting to extreme measures of looking for a "miracle cure" for Taffy, I finally realized that I had to commit my kitty to God and leave her in His hands. I had asked Rachel

Radel, one of our young ladies at St. Elias and mentioned in chapter five, to surf the Internet to see if anyone was trying new medical procedures, even if they might be considered eccentric or a bit radical. Rachel is interested in veterinary medicine and has won many first place science awards over the years. Rachel did her best but found no new innovations which would help our Taffers. Brenda said to me, "Honey, don't you think that if there was something out there available for Taffy's situation, Dr. Salzmann and his staff would know about it?" I did, but I was desperate, and desperate people often resort to extreme measures. I had to try for Taffy.

However, being a Christian, I knew that the best thing and the logical thing to do was to commit my feline friend to God. I also had to seek His will and what was best for her. If God decided to heal Taffy that would be wonderful, and if not, well that would have to do and in its own way it would be wonderful too.

This is what we believers need to do: put everything in God's care and trust in Him completely. We can be sure that He has our best interests at heart. He is looking out for us every day, providing, preparing and planning our future, Jeremiah 29:11. Our part is to obey and follow Him and make Him the number one priority in our lives. He should be our "Senior Partner" in all our endeavors of life. So, we put Taffy at God's disposal—after all, she really belongs to Him, not to us. He created her and the fact of the matter is, everyone and everything is His as the God of the universe. The Apostle Paul reminds us,

You are not your own. You were bought with a price. So then glorify God with your body (1 Corinthians 6:19-20).

The "price" was the precious blood of His own dear Son, Jesus Christ, 1 Peter 1:18-21. He made the ultimate sacrifice, He was the "Divine Victim" of the world's most infamous atrocity in the history of mankind. If we want to know how bad human beings can be, we only need to look to the Cross. There, the only perfect and completely innocent Person who walked the face of the earth was mocked, humiliated, and crucified! And He said in the midst of it all, "Father, forgive them..." And that is the ultimate, most stupendous expression of love this old world has ever seen. That is the kind of God I can love and trust.

PRAYERS FOR A PUSSYCAT

I was deeply moved by the loving response of so many people who shared their concern with us about Taffy's condition. My prayer group I mentioned before, which meets every Friday at 6:00 a.m., is composed of fine Christian men who hold one another up in love and prayer. I referred to Bob Reich, our leader, and Tom Gresh before and how they supported and encouraged us. Foster Furman, our oldest member at ninety-plus and patriarch of Furman Foods, offered me guidance and suggestions in the writing of Cats I, and serious prayer in this situation with our kitty. Homer Klock, one of our St. Elias members—and one of the "persons" owned by Kitten, chapter one—gave so much care and prayer. The other great guys, Bud Smith, Marlin Bohner, Al Scholl, Maurice Reichard, George Stahl, Eric Michael, George Halama, Corey Furman, and some more fellows remembered us in prayer and in Christian love. These are more of those wonderful people I spoke of in the previous chapter.

Of course, my terrific folks at Zion and St. Elias consented to pray for the Taffers and Brenda and I in this time of distress. Christian friends who heard about it or those with whom we shared our concern also gave their empathy and promises of prayer. All the cat lovers we know certainly understood our pain and offered helpful suggestions, and many said that they would pray for us and Taffy. People that we do not know and even some we have never met told members and friends that they were praying for Taffy. Some churches added her to their prayer list. I didn't do that at my own churches, although I did ask for prayer from those who had no problem with praying for a pet. We were overwhelmed with the concern and the support we received.

As we continued to monitor Taffy's trips to the litter box, we noticed a gradual increase in her urine output as time went on. We watched her carefully to try to see if she was in pain and terrible discomfort. We periodically checked with Dr. Salzmann and the folks at the animal hospital for advice and reassurance. We wanted to make sure that we were doing right with our Taffy. We wanted to give the best possible care to our little girl. She has given so much to us and we are thankful to God for giving her to us. We love this courageous feline "trooper."

TOUCHING MOMENTS

One Saturday evening in November, I called my mother as I usually always do on the weekend and was joined by my convalescent kitty on the bed. I made my call at eight o'clock and talked to Mom until nine, using my free weekends from the phone company. I keep close tabs on her because of her health and because I love my mother dearly. I feel sorry for people who do not have a good, loving relationship with their parents—or their families too, for that matter. Life is too brief to miss the magic moments it affords during our tenure on this old earth. We should cherish our God-given time with loved ones and spend as much of it with them as we can. I live 55 miles from Mom, but I go to see her as often as possible. Often, I take Brenda and Mary along, and we take Mom out for lunch. It's good to get the "Grandmas" together.

Well, I was no sooner on the bed than a multi-colored kitty was up with me purring profusely and wanting my undivided attention. I was lying on my side, propped up on some pillows talking to Mom, and my furry pal laid down beside me, looking lovingly into my face with dreamy eyes. The entire hour Taffy stayed with me lying mostly on her side and staring at me as I carried on my conversation via the phone. I became aware of another conversation that was taking place as I spoke with Mom. My kitty was being communicative with eye contact and body language. I don't think she took her eyes off me for five minutes. This pretty baby rolled over on her back holding her front paws in a curled up position, all the while watching me and blinking her eyes as if to keep my attention.

If I happened to look away, a front paw reached out and touched my hand or arm to let me know that I was not doing my part to maintain the conversation. Actually, she would touch me from time to time just—I think—as an expression of her love for me. Taffy was thoroughly enjoying this time together and so was I, realizing that her time might be short and knowing that every minute was precious. Not once during this time did she get down to go to the litter box or eat or drink. She continued to purr the entire hour, seemingly content and quite happy. I don't think that she meowed, even softly, once during this hour but kept on purring her patented nasal purr she was known for. I am not going to say that Taffy and I bonded that night because I feel we established a close connection a long time ago. This time together just reinforced my realization and awareness of our special relationship. I don't know how many times that evening I thanked the Lord for my wonderful kitty.

MORE KITTY KARE NEEDED

I am amazed at how our little purr puppy continued to follow her natural instincts even in the face of such a serious condition. Not once did she resort to urinating outside the litter box, although we wouldn't have blamed her in this situation. I can't help but believe she did this out of consideration for us. Love and training are much more effective than people realize, including many pet owners. When a pet is more than a pet, the animal senses the love and how important he is to his person or people. It makes a difference as any serious and dedicated pet owner will attest. Brenda and I have established a very unique relationship with our two "buddies" and I hope that message is getting across.

A problem did arise when Taffy was sleeping, however, and my life partner was quick to respond with a logical solution. She had less control over her bladder while she was asleep, and so we took measures to accommodate the "leaky" kitty. Brenda put plastic over the mattresses on the beds, over chairs, in the pet taxis, or anywhere she napped. The Tassers didn't seem to mind the arrangement, and it worked well to prevent a lot of urine soaked items. She did have a few accidents while we were lying down or sleeping with her, but we just washed our clothes and whatever else was wet. Our laundry increased during this time, and I was concerned about the extra electric and oil expense this might cause for the parsonage. So I made a donation to the churches' joint account which our treasurer was reluctant to accept. However, I try to be fair, especially where the Lord's business is concerned.

With my ministry, I could not spend every waking moment with Taffy, although it seemed that she wanted more attention as the condition progressed. When I worked in the study, she would come in and want some love and attention. I desperately wanted to oblige her but I knew I had to get my work done. So I brought in a chair and put a small cushion on it, and I sat Taffy beside me. She gave it a quick inspection, then curled up and took a nap. She seemed content with my accommodation, and looked for the chair whenever she came into the study. I felt so good to have her want to be with me.

TAFFY'S CONDITION GROWS WORSE

We noticed our little girl slowing down and cutting back on her eating and drinking. She would sit about a foot or so away from the dishes and just stare at them. We tried to give her small amounts of tuna and let her lick soft food off our fingers. At least that way we were getting some nourishment in her.

Her breathing seemed different and she purred more quietly. We also detected a sharp twitch, especially when she was sleeping, making us wonder if it was caused by pain. We didn't want to think about it, but we knew we couldn't ignore it and must do what was best for Taffy. She also had trouble jumping up on the bed in our room. The bed is an old iron rail-type and is very high, and it became difficult for her to leap up. Brenda suggested taking it apart and just laying the springs and the mattress on the floor. The kitty had no problem ascending the much lower bed, and we were relieved that we made something easier for her.

We continued to give her lactulose to make sure her bowels were working, and we tried a bit of laxatone from time to time. It seemed that she fought us even more and more when we gave her the medicine and this broke our hearts. It was hard on us, but we carefully got as much lactulose in her as we could. We didn't want her to have problems with being bound up as well as the cancer.

TIME FOR A DECISION

One morning, I went upstairs after breakfast and saw Brenda watching Taffy sitting in front of the food dishes. My wife had tears in her eyes and she said, "We have to do something." We talked for a while and decided at that point to make some front paw prints of our kitty. She did not appreciate this too much but we wanted them so badly and we got some good ones.

After acquiring the paw prints, Taffy jumped up on the cedar chest beside me and staggered a bit. Brenda said, "Clair, look at her eyes." Through my tears I examined my baby cat's eyes and saw that they looked cloudy. Our kitty did not feel good. I said to Brenda, "Call the animal hospital and talk to Darlene." I was referring to Darlene Reffeor, a long-time staff member of the hospital and a good Christian friend.

Brenda was not up to making the call, so I phoned and asked for Darlene. I explained the situation to her and that we felt it was time to have Taffy evaluated. I told Darlene that we thought we knew it might be time to make the dreaded decision. I asked if she could make an appointment for us with Dr. Salzmann as early as possible. Darlene informed us that he was in surgery at the time I called, but that she would check with him for a time. Around noon, Darlene called back and told us to bring Taffy in at 7:30 a.m. the next day. After hanging up the phone, I told Brenda the news and we hugged and cried.

THE NIGHT BEFORE

Needless to say, there were three heavy hearts in the Shaffer home. Mary, Brenda's mother and an avowed non-cat lover who was being won over slowly, was as concerned as were we. Tiffy especially, had done much to change Mary's attitude toward cats. Not threatened by Mary's presence at all, the Tiffers accepted her and went about business as usual. My mother-in-law began to be impressed by the little one's cute antics and became quite fond of "Puss Cat" as she calls her. Mary didn't see much of Taffy as she did not accept our new resident, as I mentioned before. Yet, when Mary did see her, she talked to her and tried to get Miss Multi-Colored to come into the living room and join the family. For some reason, known really only to Taffy, she refused to give in and make friends with Mary. Mary was touched by the situation with our kitty, knowing how we felt about her.

After doing some afternoon visitation, I went upstairs to Taffy and spent some time with her before supper. Then after the meal, I went back up and gave the rest of the evening to my special friend. She was delighted! In the afternoon, Brenda had spent every possible minute with her. Talk about precious moments!

I sat on the edge of the bed and talked with Tassy, petting and stroking her, rubbing that belly—her favorite form of affection—and just smothered her with love. Of course, she ate it up! She purred and answered me when I talked to her most of the time. Again, I received strokes and touches of affection from little white front paws reaching out to make contact with me. In the course of the evening, she got down to use the litter box and eat or drink, but she came right back.

I kept my box of tissues nearby, and my furry companion sensed that I was having a problem. After some time had passed, if Taffy left, when she returned she laid her head on my leg and looked up into my face. She wanted to get as close to me as she could. I kept praying and thanking God for this love-bug kitty and the nearly 15 years we had her. The tears continued to flow and the tissues continued to disappear from the box. During these five or six hours, I realized just how much I loved Taffy, just how much I would miss her if…! I dismissed the thought from my mind. I knew that I had always loved her, but in time of crisis, we usually become more cognizant of our affection for a loved one. In fact, my mother had realized this and said to Brenda, "I'm really worried about Bud! If something happens to Taffy, I don't think he could handle it." My dear wife tried to reassure her that her son was tougher than he appeared on the outside. The only reason for my "toughness" is the Lord. He gets me through the tough times.

At one point during the evening, Taffy got down and went over to the closet, laid down on her side and stuck a paw under the door to try to open it. This went on for a while and then I baby-talked her back to the bed where she laid back down with her head on my knee, looking dreamy-eyed into my face. I remembered that she had gone into the closet not too long ago when I forgot to close the door and burrowed into some old beat-about clothes in the far end corner. It took us a while to find her because Taffy does not usually give herself away, and we did not notice the ajar door right away. When we did locate her, we actually had to go in the closet and carry her out because she wouldn't budge on her own. As I sat now on the bed, petting her and talking to her, it occurred to me that perhaps she was looking for a secluded place to die. An animal knows instinctively when it's life is in danger, and often it looks for a private place to expire. I wondered if this was what my kitty was doing. More tears, more tissues.

Ironically, all the time during the evening as we sat together on the bed, Taffy did not urinate on the covers. But then, she didn't fall asleep, and that was when she seemed to lose control. My little lady was so considerate, retiring each time to the litter box and returning to me. Each time she did have an "accident," we used moistened wipes to clean her up and also sprayed some "Pet Groom" on our hands and rubbed it on her. This spray is harmless to pets and has a pleasing aroma that eliminates urine and litter box odors for some time.

Later Brenda came upstairs after helping Mary get ready for bed. She had, from time to time, come up to peek in on Taffy and me to see how we were doing. Now, she came in and sat down with us on the bed and talked to the pussycat and petted and kissed her. Then my wife had a great suggestion. "Should we see if Tassy wants to go downstairs?" she said to me, but within the kitty's hearing. No sooner were the words out of her mouth than Miss Multi-Colored was staring at her with bright eyes and perked ears. I got up and said, "Does Tassy want to go downstairs?" With that I headed on down and Brenda called to me, "Daddy, look behind you." Not far from my heels I heard a thump, thump, thump, and upon looking back, I saw Taffy following closely down the steps.

I went into the back room and sat down on the sofa. I was joined immediately by my furry friend who laid down beside me and began purring, apparently very happy and content. Brenda came out into the room and we talked with her and made much ado over her—all of it real and sincere. It is easy for us to make a fuss over Taffy because we love her so much. All the while we were in the back room, she didn't become apprehensive or show any signs of worry like she normally did when she was downstairs. It was uncanny just how calm she was, seemingly oblivious to her usual concerns about Mary being there or other people showing up at the house.

Brenda came up with another idea and said, "Daddy, do you think that Taffy would like to go into the living room?" I answered, "I don't know, Mommy—let's see if Taffers wants to check out all the stuff in the front room and the living room." I got up and started for the living room, looked back at Taffy who was still lying on the sofa and said, "Come on, Snooker-doos, let's go and see Mommy's stuff." Like a flash she was off the couch and right behind me as I went into the back living room.

She waltzed in as if she owned the place, oozing calm and confidence that I have rarely seen in Taffy in situations like this. Brenda said, "Do you believe this cat?" I looked at my wife and said, "I know—it's really scary." I walked on into the front living room and sat down on the floor. Without an invitation, our kitty strutted into the room and right up to me, and I kissed her on the head and petted her and said to her, "What do you think, Tassy?" As if accommodating my question, she looked around and went over to the French doors to Mary's bedroom—which Brenda had closed previously in preparation of this plan—and sort of peeked between the doors to make sure that the elder resident was safely tucked away for the night. Brenda had also told Mary what she had planned to do so that she would know what was going on if she heard voices downstairs and saw some lights on.

After checking out Mary's status and being content that she would cause no interference, Taffy began inspecting items in the room, especially the fire engine kiddie car and the Radio Flyer wagon with wood sides, both of which were filled with stuffed animals. We suspected that she sneaked down at night and checked things out, but now she acted as if she was seeing these things for the first time. Never once, after her initial check on Mary, did she seem apprehensive or frightened while on her tour of the downstairs. The wooden "kittie car" I had made for them got the once-over as well as the stuffed animals Brenda neatly arranged within it. All other plush critters received the same treatment as did some more items in the room. Following her careful inspection of the area, she laid down in the middle of the floor in a patented Taffy-position, and purred up a storm, quite happy and content.

We sat with her for a while, talking to her and petting her, and just enjoying the company of this incredible cat. Then Brenda said, "Tassy, let's look in the other room—okay?" With that, we walked to the rear living room and sat down on the floor, followed by Miss Three-tone who began scrutinizing the contents of this room. She observed all the stuffed animals within her reach and investigated anything that seemed new since she had been there before. She plopped down and started to purr, all the while looking back and forth to Brenda and I, indubitably happy to be with us like in times of old. It brought back a host of memories.

When my sensible mate recommended that we head up to bed, I reluctantly agreed, not wanting this moment to end. But I knew that our early morning appointment would come quickly and we both would need some sleep. I picked Taffy up—without any protest from her—and carried her upstairs. I fixed up a place for her on the bed and Brenda prepared to sleep in the spare bedroom. She wanted the Tassers to bunk with Daddy since he usually sacks out in his recliner downstairs due to all the digestive problems. My kitty stayed with me for a while, but when I woke up soon after dozing off, she had left. I did manage to get some sleep despite what might transpire the following day.

THE APPOINTMENT

My alarm went off at five a.m. and I quickly arose, wanting to get started right away with my shower and preparations for the day. I wanted to locate Taffy so I would know where she was if we needed to round her up, but I also wanted to say good morning to her. I didn't find her right away, and I was quiet, not wishing to disturb Brenda that early. When I checked the water dish in the spare bedroom, I looked up to see her lying on the gossip bench, all curled up. I leaned over, kissed her on the head, and whispered good morning to her. By this time, Brenda was stirring, and she also said a soft "good morning" to our beloved kitty.

After my spouse took a shower and got ready for the day, she went downstairs to tend to Mary. I was in the bathroom upstairs making sure everything was in order, like the commode lid being in the down position, and any small items dangerous to a cat being safely put away. It was about ten of seven when the phone rang. On the other end of the line was Terry Latsha, one of the elders at our St. Elias Church. If I remember correctly, Terry was calling from his mother, Ruby's home, where he stops every morning on his way to work to check on her and do things for her. Ruby is legally blind as I mentioned in a previous chapter, but lives alone and functions very proficiently. Her family loves her dearly and, like good Christian sons and daughters, respect her independence but are there for her in every way. Terry, a very caring person, called to see how Brenda and I were doing, knowing the time of our appointment with Dr. Salzmann at the animal hospital. He said to me, "Are you guys okay? Do you need someone else to go with you?" He wasn't embarrassed when I broke down—he and wife, Pam, had been there, too. I thanked him and told him how much we appreciated the offer, but that we would be okay. Brenda and I were moved, impressed with Terry's concern. Aren't God's people great?

We put Taffy in her pet taxi as gently as we could, baby-talking her all the time, attempting to calm and reassure our darling. Downstairs we let Mary see her, and my mother-in-law had some trouble handling the situation. She knew the seriousness of our kitty's condition and had to make a similar trip years ago with their puppy, Mitzi, who was nearly 19 years old. Taffy was bright-eyed, quite a contrast to the bleary look she had for the past couple of weeks. She knew that when we put her in the carrier more often than not the destination was the animal hospital. Both our kitties seem to have the "white coat syndrome," a term applied to people who have a fear of doctors. As soon as we walked in the door and she smelled the scents of the clinic, she knew where she was.

We were greeted by Darlene Reffeor, a good friend and a Christian, who is the head receptionist at the hospital. Darlene has worked there for over 30 years and is one of those caring individuals who does her best to help others through any painful situation. We checked in and did not have to wait long before Dr. Salzmann summoned us into one of the exam rooms. Brenda and I walked in and exchanged our hellos with Dr. Salzmann and his assistant,

Stacey Balliet, and we were still holding on to some faint glimmer of hope.

We lifted Taffy out of her pet taxi and set her down on the little cover Stacey had placed on the examining table. Her eyes were still big and bright as we petted her and talked to her. Dr. Salzmann said hello to her, stroked and caressed her, and talked to her in a soothing, soft voice. Then, he began his examination, noticing particularly the bladder tumor, and the effect it had upon her system. He listened to her heart and checked her over thoroughly. He checked her side and belly once more and said, "It's time—the tumor has really progressed." Then he leaned down to Taffy and said softly, "We're going to stop this pain, Baby, we're going to make it better." Brenda and I lost it! Stacey had gone out to get the necessary medication and returned with a box of tissues. We had stuffed our pockets and Brenda's pocketbook with a pile of them, but they were fast being used up. I noticed that the good doctor and Stacey were also having some problems, and they availed themselves of the tissues as well.

I made mention of this and Dr. Salzmann said, "I console myself in that I am ending their pain and suffering. That is the only way I can handle it and get through." I thought of the many times he had to "get through" having to share the emotional trauma of his clients and mercifully bring a beloved pet's life to an end. It takes a special person to perform such a task with empathy and kindness—a person who truly cares about the pet and its people. Dr. Salzmann is one of those special persons.

The first procedure was to give an injection of anesthesia to Taffy to render her unconscious. This was given in the thigh. Dr. Salzmann explained everything as he went along, and we appreciated knowing just what was happening to our kitty. The anesthesia would knock her out, of course, and slow down the heart and body system, preparing it for the medication which would finally shut it down. I never knew about the anesthesia; I had thought that an injection was given to the pet and it went to sleep. This would be too traumatic, as Dr. Salzmann explained, and could cause undue suffering. Thus, the anesthesia prepared the pet for the final injection.

Brenda and I had been petting and kissing Taffy all along but were a bit remiss in our show of affection as Dr. Salzmann talked with us. Our thoughts were centered upon what he was saying, and so after he administered the anesthesia, Stacey said to us, "You can pet her and talk to her if you want to." That snapped us out of our lethargic state, and we were glad because we wanted to spend every one of her last waking moments telling her and showing her how much we loved her. We were happy that Stacey brought us back to reality.

As we talked with Taffy and showered her with love, Brenda was more in front of her than I was and remarked about her big eyes. I commented that she did not look dreary-eyed now. About this time, Dr. Salzmann checked her and said that she was out. Brenda said, "No, her eyes are open." Then Stacey explained that animals do not close their eyes when under anesthesia or when they die. While undergoing surgery, technicians must moisten their eyes continually to prevent them from drying out. We never knew this and had thought that animals closed their eyes like humans while under anesthesia.

We continued to wipe away the tears as Dr. Salzmann prepared the final injection of pentobarbital to stop Taffy's heart and bring her precious existence on earth to an end. It was so surreal—as if this was not really happening. We had heard about other's experiences in putting down a pet, saw such stories on TV, and I had read many accounts of the trauma that cat and dog lovers went through when the dreaded day came. Now it was happening to us! Brenda and I didn't try to hide our grief. Dr. Salzmann used his stethoscope to make his final judgment. Taffy was gone! All four of us stood there for a while in silence, still sort of stunned by the moment. I silently prayed for help.

After telling Dr. Salzmann that we wanted to have Taffy cremated, he and Stacey left the exam room to allow us to have a few minutes alone with our kitty. We wept, hugged each other, hugged and kissed our Tassy, and petted her one last time. Our good doctor friend then returned and asked us if we would like a clip of her hair. We were so glad that he thought of it and said that we certainly would like that, and thanked him for his kindness and help. After shaking hands and asking Dr. Salzmann to thank Stacey for us, we went out to the lobby to offer our gratitude to Darlene for her kind help as well. As we were about ready to leave, I turned around just in time to see Dr. Salzmann carry Taffy through the hallway behind the reception desk. She was lying on the cover and looked so peaceful. It would be the final time that I would see my little friend—at least here on earth.

It was a long ride home, all three quarters of a mile of it, but one of the most lengthy trips I'm sure that we ever made. We walked in the house somewhat like zombies, and said very little to Mary, who no doubt would have choked up. We both went upstairs with me carrying the empty pet taxi—a very somber feeling indeed. Tiffany was hiding because we had taken her sister out in the carrier. Brenda and I chose not to disturb her. We cried and hugged some more and tried to eat some breakfast and ease into the routine of the day.

SOME REFLECTIONS

After learning of Taffy's condition back in October, I decided to be practical and prepare for the worst all the while hoping for the best. I went up to the garage and picked some nice lumber and built a casket for our treasured furry friend. I took extra care to seal and stain the wood because at the time I wasn't just sure what I wanted to do with regard to her body. I did talk with David Blank, a friend I mentioned before who is a mortician, about having Taffy embalmed or something! David said that he had never embalmed an animal but that his father, Jerre, had performed the process on a friend's pet dog. Jerre's aunt, Jane Wetzel, a retired mortician, told me that Jerre's friend ordered a full-fledged funeral for his dog. Jane and husband, Glenn, live right next door to Jerre's Sunbury funeral home and this wonderful lady still helps out at viewings, greeting people and consoling them. Although Glenn and Jane are not official members of our Zion Church, they attended for many years until health problems interrupted their life style. They feel very blessed to have David, his wife, Nicole, and sons, Spencer and Toby, living right next to them above the funeral parlor. Those little guys are the apple of their eyes.

Well, I did not wish to be that eccentric—have a complete funeral for Taffy. I felt odd enough just asking about embalming her. However, David and Bob Radel, from our St. Elias congregation, suggested taxidermy instead since there is no decay. This, I gave some very serious thought to because I could choose any position to lay her in the casket and look in on her whenever I wished. I surmised that I could have the taxidermist place her in a sleeping position and then arrange her favorite toys around her. It would be like having her still in my life. This bubble burst when Brenda told me that she could not handle it. I thought I could change her mind, but my wife would not budge. And everyone else took her side. Many pet owners tried to convince me that I would regret it but I am still not convinced. However, I finally acquiesced and gave in to cremation.

About ten days after we had Taffy put to sleep, our friend Darlene from the animal hospital called to tell us that they had her ashes. We went down immediately and Darlene brought out a red tin in the shape of an old chest. We opened it and found that Taffy's ashes were in a plastic bag. Neither of us knew just how this was handled, not having been involved with cremation before. The ashes, incredibly, looked gray, white and beige, our Calico's colors, and Brenda lost it. I was able to maintain my composure a bit better, but it was difficult. We thanked Darlene, Donna, Jackie, Beverly, and Jessica for all their help and sympathy. We were very appreciative of the nice card and ceramic plaque they sent us in memory of Taffy. The plaque, white with a red rose on it, has this nice saying:

> *In Memory of Taffy*
> The pet we loved will remain with us forever,
> and cherished memories will abide within our
> hearts, reminding us that the love we shared
> together is eternal.

For fourteen years and nine months, these nice caring people had attended to our kitty's needs with love and finesse. We were so very grateful for all they had done. They will continue to care for our Tiffany whom we hope will be around for many more years.

The day after Taffy went to "kitty heaven"—or just heaven as I truly believe, although I cannot prove it from Scripture—Brenda, Mary, and I went out to eat at a local restaurant. I was doing fairly well until the music system began to play a Kenny Roger's song, "Through The Years." The melody and the lyrics just reminded me of Taffy and all the wonderful times we had with her down through the years. I leaned over to Brenda and said, "I'll be back," as the tears welled up in my eyes, and I hurried to the restroom. In there I slowly regained my composure and returned to my seat. My loving partner told me that the song hit her, too, but this time she was able to stay in control while I could not. Other songs would affect us as well and no doubt always will. Both of us are easily emotionally moved, and it does not take much to moisten our eyes.

What can I say about Taffy that I have not already said? What words can be used to describe a beautiful little cat who brought so much love and joy to a pastor and his wife for nearly 15 years? I like to think that she touched many more lives than just ours—those who have heard about her, meaning people close to us, and thousands more who have read about her. Is it possible for the world to be a better place because a small furry feline graced it with her presence for a few years? I believe so, especially if God sent her as a diminutive ambassador of His glory and good will. How many pet owners will attest to that? I am convinced that our loving heavenly Father delights in utilizing His charming and fascinating creatures to influence us "higher order class of animals." As I said in Cats I, we can learn so much. I have never been impressed by a pet as I have with Taffy. I don't know what her cat IQ was, but I am sure it was very high. I tell people that I think she understood 90% of what we said to her. Scary? Eerie? Unusual? Unique? Incredible? Amazing? All of the above and more! I said before that she was a special cat. But then who created her?

THANK YOU AGAIN, FATHER, FOR TAFFY!

I hear people, especially Christians, giving thanks to God for individuals who have helped them or made a positive impact on their lives. This is proper and biblical. Consider the Apostle Paul's words to the believers at Philippi: "I thank my God upon every remembrance of you" (Philippians 1:3).

I cannot possibly count the many people that God has sent into my life and is still sending in His wisdom and grace. I thank Him for each one and I pray that I have been of some inspiration and encouragement to them as they have been to me. Our heavenly Father knows just who to send into our lives and when. I still marvel at His intervention in our lives and the divine designs He has for all of us. I can't wait to see what He is going to do next!

In the same way, I am amazed and thrilled at the many wonderful pets He has brought across the paths of our lives. I was privileged to have three dogs of my own—Tiny, Figsie, and my boxer, Rinny. My only cat before my wife and I were married was Tiffany, a Siamese. I did not do justice to these wonderful friends because back then I did not know what I know now about pets. Over the years I have had the pleasure of meeting some great cats and dogs, some I mentioned in Cats I and earlier in this book. I am indebted to the Lord for every one I got to know. Each had their own special personality which made them unique.

And if we are talking about personality, our little Taffy was Miss Personality Plus. She walked like a model, oozing confidence as she placed one foot in front of the other. I never saw a cat walk that way before with such a deliberate gait. It's as if someone told her, "Walk like you are a big VIP, someone special, a real dignitary." To us, of course, she was, and we told her so—over and over. Taffy was a take charge person—er, pussycat—who sort of demanded your attention when she came into the room. She announced herself with a distinctive "meow," which meant, of course, "Okay! I'm here, so drop what you're doing and listen up!" That little twerp commanded some regard with her authoritative meow.

And we usually stopped what we were doing and accommodated our multi-colored friend. I wonder if she didn't intimidate us with her air of importance. It sounds funny, doesn't it, but there was just something about Taffy that caught your attention and drew you to her. Her magnetic personality was difficult to resist, and most times we gave in to our kitty's whims. Now, I am glad we did.

I hope that I am right in believing that we will see Taffy again in heaven and be with her forever. I cannot prove from the Bible that our pets will be in heaven, nor can I disprove it. Some theologians are definite in their claims that animals will be included in the realm of glory. Often Ecclesiastes 3:21 is quoted as proof that animals will not enter into Eternity:

Who can be sure that the spirit of a man ascends upward, or if the spirit of an animal descends down into the earth?"

Now, this text does not prove either view, whether we translate it as it is above or as follows:

Who can know the spirit of a man, which ascends upward, or the spirit of an animal which descends into the earth?"

The meaning is not affected in either case, and we cannot establish a doctrine from this passage. One of the rules of Hermeneutics—the science of biblical interpretation—is that you do not establish or teach doctrine from poetry. The Book of Ecclesiastes is poetry and was written by King Solomon from the worldly man's point of view. The man of the world—those who make wealth, a career, or pleasure the priority of their lives, many times see life as "meaningless, meaningless...everything is meaningless!" This phrase is used by Solomon over and over in Ecclesiastes to describe the reasoning of someone who majors on things that have no permanent value. Thus we cannot draw a conclusion about the fate of our pets from a book of the Bible—although divinely inspired—which presents the view of the unspiritual man.

In my belief that our pets will be in heaven, I am basing my faith in God's love for His creatures who are very special to Him. Although they have been affected by man's original sin, they are basically innocent—more innocent than we human beings. As one little boy said, "They do not have to live as long as we do. It takes us a lot of time to learn to love each other and get along. They already know how to do that!" What a thought! Oh why can't we learn?

And so I thank the Lord for sending Taffy into our lives. I am grateful too, to that little kitty for all the love and the lessons she taught us. Sorry Taffy, that it took so long for me to learn some of them. Now we treasure the memories of this fantastic feline who touched us with an indelible charm we will never forget. I often ask myself now, was I worthy of this little angel sent from God?

CHAPTER 7

NEW YORK CITY!

Oh, the places that our cats have taken us and the adventures that we have experienced! In December my publisher asked me if Brenda and I would like to come to New York City to a Book Expo. He explained that I would be autographing copies of *Cats in the Parsonage* for several hours during the show. There would be several thousand publishers present in the Jacob Javits Center, with many authors promoting their books. It sounded like the opportunity of a lifetime. Right away I thought of the cost and began doubting whether we could swing it or not. I recently had some auto repair bills that depleted our extra cash reserve and I was feeling the pinch. "O ye of little faith!" How soon we forget!

Like the Israelites of old, we quickly fail to remember the miraculous blessings of the Lord and become doubtful and afraid. I had to remind myself how God wonderfully provided the funds to publish my first book.

Although I still have a lot of work to do on myself—an inferiority complex to some extent, self-doubt, lack of confidence, and other negative personality traits—the Lord helped me take a big step in the right direction in correcting these debilitating flaws. I should have been believing, trusting, and receiving His blessings and benefits all along, but I blocked their flow because of my disbelief. "And He could not perform many miracles because of their lack of faith" (Matthew 13:58).

This was said in Jesus' own hometown of Nazareth where perhaps He should have been welcomed with open arms and pride in a local "Boy" who made good. Talk about a hero returning home! No one ever accomplished what He did—so much good for the entire human race for every person who has ever lived, is living now, or will live—in three years! And all He asks is that we believe! We cancel out His blessings by our disbelief. Remember those lies we tell ourselves: "God will never do that for me; I don't deserve it; I am not good enough; I don't have what it takes" and so on! Phooey! God has given us talents, abilities, and if we are Christians, supernatural spiritual gifts. Let's quit lying to ourselves and do something positive and constructive by taking God at His Word!

I decided that it was time for me to practice what I preach. To help myself and my people by being a better example of what the Lord can do with us and for us if we believe. I knew it was time for a complete "attitude overhaul." Yes, it might take some time, those old ingrained negative thoughts had a lot of time to grow and take deep root. They would have to be displaced and replaced with new, positive, and healthy thoughts on a regular basis. Paul talks about "thought replacement" in Philippians 4:8, when he tells us to think about things that are "true, noble, right, pure, lovely, worthy, exemplary and deserving of praise." Who could get into trouble thinking about thing like these? In any event, I was on my way, determined to shed this inferiority complex and open my heart open wide to receive God's blessings.

MAKING PLANS

Brenda and I weren't quite sure how we were going to pull this trip off with her mother, Mary, living with us and needing continual care. Now, Mary is far from being an invalid, but we would never go and leave her alone for a few days. In the house she gets around with a wheelchair and a walker and does well. However, due to arthritis she is a little wobbly on her feet, so we hesitate to go away for any extended periods of time. In finding someone to stay with her, we agreed that my mom was the logical and best choice since they both get along together fine; my mom knows our home, having stayed with us before, and handles problems well; and she is acquainted with our church families and can answer parish questions should someone call; and very importantly—she likes cats and would not mind taking care of our little sweeties. Of course, when the time came to go to New York, Taffy was gone, so Mom had only one kitty to take care of.

I spoke to my Mom about this idea and she was ecstatic that we had this great opportunity. The only roadblock might come in the form of cancer treatment should her lymphoma require attention. She was to see her Oncologist about a month before our trip. Otherwise, she was willing to do it, wanting Brenda and I to go to the Big Apple. We committed her and our plans to the Lord.

Mom received good news at her checkup, and we were all delighted. On May 5th Brenda and I would celebrate our 20th anniversary, and we had not been away since our wedding. The timing seemed perfect. We could spend our anniversary in New York City! Our excitement grew even more intense as we thought of the possibility. Personally, I thought, "Can this be happening to me?" See! Old habits are difficult to break. When you are used to failing and have convinced yourself that you'll "never make it," success sometimes is hard to accept and digest. But I had a good feeling about this, and I put everything in the Lord's trustworthy hands.

As the time grew near, we incurred some unexpected expenses and had to use some of our money for the trip. I told Brenda, "We're not going to become concerned. This is God's will, I'm convinced of it, and He is going to provide the means for going to New York." Not long after that, I received a royalty check, which would more than cover any cost of our excursion to the Big Apple. We both said a hearty "thank you" to our heavenly Father.

It was hard not to pack early and refrain from taking too much stuff. We were excited, but decided to use some discretion and carefully chose the items we would really need. Brenda and I are great for lists and we use them for just about everything. I kid people that I need lists to remind me of my lists. We use them all over the house and in the cars. I have forgotten too many important things to take chances, especially in my ministry. So we made up a list of things we would take on the trip. Included in our roster was a few phone numbers for Mom to call should she need to ask for help. Besides people in the church, we listed our oil company, the electric company, our plumber, the local hospital, and so on.

We knew that my dear mother would have no trouble taking care of Mary or Tiffany. She was feeling very good and was looking forward to spending time at the parsonage. I'm sure it gave her a change of pace and scenery—a break from her usual routine. Brenda and I really appreciated it to say the least! We made sure that our two precious ladies had everything they needed and more!

PASTOR...START YOUR ENGINE!

The Lord blessed our attempts to make reservations in the big city far beyond our expectations. I stopped at our local AAA Auto Club and the fine folks there mapped out the best route for us and gave us helpful information. As we were looking through the booklets on hotels and motels, my astute, eagle-eye wife spotted one right above the Lincoln Tunnel, two blocks from the Jacob Javits Convention Center. We made the call and they had one room left! We were only interested in one night, but to secure the room we had to take it for two nights. It did not take long for us to say yes because we decided that we deserved it. It was the weekend of our anniversary, and we were finally getting away after 20 years.

We were able to reserve the room and were given a ten dollar a night discount because we were participants at the Book Expo. We hugged, kissed, and praised the Lord! Every step of the way, He made our plans fall into place and provided for our needs. These two novice travelers were so thankful.

The departure date rolled around and we were up super early, wanting to get on the road by seven a.m. It was a bright, beautiful sunny morning and we were excited to get going. We had packed most of our stuff the night before and so we started out right at seven o'clock. After stopping briefly at a donut shop in nearby Danville for coffee and goodies to go, we pulled on to Route 80 East and set the car on cruise control. We were on our way!

The interstate was in good condition and we made good time, stopping once or twice for pit stops. As we entered New Jersey, we were impressed with the emergency phones placed every so often along the highway. We both commented that our own state of Pennsylvania should consider installing these much-needed phones on our interstates. We bought a cell phone mainly for this trip, but not everyone has one.

"SKYSCRAPERS AHEAD!"

As we got closer to New York, I could see the skyline of the city in the distance. Brenda was looking over one of our maps and I called her attention to the impressive sight ahead. She said, "Wow! Isn't that neat?" and quickly took out the camera. I guess we country folk are easily impressed with what city dwellers take for granted.

We followed our route mapped out by the AAA and also watched the signs for the Lincoln Tunnel. In fact, one of the young men from our St. Elias Church, Scott Johnson, who lives and works in New York, told us to just follow the Tunnel signs. Scott's parents, Bob and Laurie, were born in the New York City area and still have family living there. Scott is going to culinary school besides working as a chef in a restaurant in the city. If possible, he was going to call us at our hotel later in the afternoon and get together for supper.

Soon, we found ourselves approaching the Lincoln Tunnel and Brenda said to me, "Are you going to be okay with this?" My wife knows that I do not like to be closed in or be "under" something. I enjoyed touring Penns Cave, an underground water cavern in Central Pennsylvania some years ago, but I did not like the thought of all that earth on top of me. Now here, it was only the Hudson River flowing over me! "All right, Lord, give me Your comfort and confidence!" I did fine! In a few minutes we were through and heading toward our hotel.

We were not sure exactly what street to follow en route to the hotel, but all of a sudden we were in New York City traffic. Talk about being closed in! I asked the Lord for help and resolved to stay calm. We traveled perhaps only two blocks and came to the street where our hotel was located. I wasn't sure which way to turn—right or left—but I had to do one or the other, and at that moment my sharp-eyed wife saw the hotel sign to the left. I was already in the process of turning right just because the main flow of traffic was going that way. When Brenda called my attention to the sign, I checked my left side mirror and saw that I could safely make a left turn. I quickly turned left and incurred some "horn honking," which we found is quite natural in the big cities.

Soon we were pulling into the entrance to the hotel, checking in, and unpacking in our room. There was a parking garage where we put our car and left it there—I wasn't about to drive in New York City if I didn't have to! The folk at the hotel were very helpful and accommodating. After a four and a half hour trip, we were hungry. Across the street we found a family restaurant which we patronized our entire stay. After lunch we went back to the hotel to freshen up and then decided to walk down to the convention center.

WHAT COMPANY WE WERE IN!

It took a short few minutes to walk to the center and we were impressed with the size of the place. Inside, the huge building was a bustle of activity and security. We checked in at one of the many reception desks and were directed upstairs to Evergreen Press' booth. On the way up we saw Leonard Nimoy's picture and site, and noticed a long line of people waiting for the famous actor/author to return. Later on, we saw Oliver North signing books and I boasted to Brenda, "I'm in pretty notorious company here." I received one of her patented glances and we continued on our way.

Soon, we located our Publisher's display and were delighted to meet Brian Banashak, his son, Jeff, and Acquisitions Director, Keith Carroll. We were glad that they were all able to be there. Brian's wife, Kathy, could not make the trip, having to stay home and tend to the business. But it was great to meet the people we had talked to over the past two years and from a good distance away. I guess it was like putting the faces with the names—or the voices! In any event, it was a real pleasure for us to be with these fine Christian people, and very exciting to be involved in such a major occasion.

We talked with the guys for a while and looked around the Expo, still a bit overwhelmed to be there, and then we walked back to the motel to rest and get ready should Scott give us a call. I know that he was looking forward to taking us around the Big Apple. We were hoping to get with him because we had not seen him for a while. Scott was just a youngster when he and his family came to St. Elias. Now, he was a grown up young man out on his own in the world's most famous city. It is a great privilege and a satisfying experience to be part of the lives of children and young people as a pastor, if only in a small way.

AROUND THE TOWN WITH SCOTT

It was about five o'clock when Scott called us at the hotel from the Lincoln Tunnel. We checked ourselves and made those last minute preparations to be sure that we had everything we needed to go out on the town. Soon we received a call that our young host was in the lobby. We went down and greeted Scott with handshakes and hugs, exchanged the usual pleasantries, and started out to enjoy the evening.

Imagine my surprise when I asked Scott where he was parked and he informed me that he did not have a car. I asked him how he got around and he told me by taxi or bus. I must have looked somewhat dazed, so Scott explained that in New York the insurance and expenses are so high it is often more sensible to use public transportation. He also has taken the subway on occasion. Brenda and I were in for a new experience.

We walked six to eight blocks to pick up a cab and saw immediately that Scott was "street smart" in calling to a taxi driver. Usually, just a hand motion was all it took to commandeer a fast moving yellow cab. I knew right away I did not like riding in big city taxi cabs. I am not one for speed and lane-changing. I was tempted to close my eyes and pray.

Scott first took us to St. Patrick's Cathedral and who would not be impressed with this magnificent edifice? I might have seen the Cathedral before back in 1970 when my senior class from Lancaster Bible College came here on our class trip. Even so, it was impressive again! From here, we walked to Central Park and through the park past the Tavern on the Green where so many celebrity events are held. We were experiencing the "aura" of New York City.

We left Central Park and took one of those yellow demolition derby vehicles to "Little Italy" where Scott had made reservations in a nice restaurant. We were given a window seat in the front and could take in the sights out in the street which was blocked off for some special event. It was bustling with activity and noise, and everyone seemed to be having a good time. The restaurant, Italian of course, was packed and was a virtual tintinabulation of conversation featuring many ethnic backgrounds. There seemed to be a wide age-range among the customers, implying an alluring appeal by the eatery. I am a people observer and this was a good place to scrutinize individuals and their behavior. Now, I do not stare, and in this case I did not neglect Brenda and Scott, but when they talked, I took advantage of the situation to scan the patrons.

Our server, a nice looking young man, apparently did not speak much English, but Scott had no trouble communicating our desires to him. Being involved in cuisine and culinary of the most exquisite type, Scott knows his way around the food business and how to interact with the partisans of restaurant management. I'm not sure what Scott ordered—definitely an Italian dish—but Brenda and I will never forget the lasagna we had. No offense to our mothers or anyone else who has treated us to some great lasagna over the years, this was by far the best. Of course, in all fairness, our lasagna was made by "real" Italian chefs.

We had a wonderful time with Scott, talking at the restaurant, reminiscing and asking him about his work and schooling and plans for the future. He had some questions for us about the churches and the folks at home, and of course, about the Cat book and the Expo. Time flies when you're having fun as the old saying goes, and before we knew it, the evening was gone. If I remember correctly, Scott had to go to work the next morning so we did not stay out too late. We truly appreciated his hospitality and thoughtfulness—he wouldn't let us pay for anything—and thoroughly enjoyed being with this fine young man.

"TO THE THEATER, OLD CHAP!"

Saturday began as a nice, bright sunny morning and we were up early to take in as much of it as we could. We were looking forward to attending the live production of *Les Miserables* at the Imperial

Theater. We had walked the few blocks to make reservations on Friday and were fortunate to acquire some box seat tickets up near the left side of the stage. This was Brenda's gift to us because our twentieth anniversary was the next day! We could think of no better way to celebrate our anniversary than to take in a Broadway musical.

Until the show at 2:00 p.m., we had a few hours to do some other things in this grand city. The activity that interested us the most was a bus tour through various sections of the Apple. The only problem was that we could not catch a bus until 10:00 a.m. and the tours lasted about four hours. The musical began at 2:00 p.m. and that would cut it too close. So we had to find something else to do on our own. The hotel folks helped us out with some brochures and also some suggestions. We decided to visit Dr. Norman Vincent Peal's church, Marble Collegiate, the oldest Protestant church in America, and then take a tour of the Empire State Building. So we took a cab to the church, and although we were unable to see the inside of the building, we took some pictures of this historical edifice and the statue of Dr. Peale outside the church. It was uplifting to see the church and a tribute to one of the most influential men in human history. I wish that I had read one of his books long ago. When I finally did, I was inspired by this spiritual man to see the Bible in a new light and claim God's promises for my very own. *Cats in the Parsonage* is a result of Dr. Peale's encouragement to me through his message and books. In appreciation, I sent a copy to Mrs. Ruth Stafford Peale, expressing my gratitude for her husband's ministry and inspirational tome. He truly was and still is, a "Minister to Millions!"

From there we walked to the Empire State Building and encountered some very stiff security inside. We had to empty our pockets of anything that caused their equipment to buzz. It was quite a hair-raising experience, but we knew that it was necessary because of 9/11. We had to wait in long lines, ride never ending elevators, and endure close quarters—but it was worth it! The view was stupendous from the observation floor—breath-taking and exhilarating. Brenda and I checked out the sights from every side. We purchased some souvenirs and then walked to Macy's Department Store.

At Macy's we enjoyed the electric atmosphere of this world-famous store. Brenda added to her stuffed animal collection by purchasing a Macy's Teddy Bear. Then, we decided it was time to head back to the hotel, grab some lunch, and get ready to take in *Les Miserables.* We flagged a cab and were at the hotel in no time flat.

It was a few blocks to the Imperial Theater, but we made it in good time and got through the lines and up to our box seats. There were five chairs in the mezzanine and we had been informed that there may be some other people joining us. However, no one else showed up, so we had it all to ourselves. The theater was impressive—beautifully constructed and adorned—and we sat in awe, wondering just how many command performances were presented within its historic walls over the years.

Soon the musical was under way and we knew immediately that we had made a good choice. The cast were super talented actors and singers, and we were caught up in the spirit of the drama of *Les Miserables.* Throughout the musical, we laughed and cried, listened intently, and reveled in the blessing of being there. How God had directed and provided in every aspect of this trip to New York City! At the end of the musical, we stood with the overflow crowd and gave the players the ovation they deserved. We didn't want to let them go, and they accommodated us with one curtain call after another.

From the theater, we walked to our favorite restaurant for supper and enjoyed a slice of delicious New York Cheese Cake. It was a splurge, but we thought we don't get to the Big Apple every day. We wanted to make the most of our trip. That evening we took a walk, relaxed, and checked in at home. Mom answered the phone, of course, and assured us that everything was all right. She and Mary were having no problems, and several of our parishioners called or stopped by to say hello and see how things were going. Mom then had to tell me about our kitty. Early that morning, five o'clock a.m. to be exact, she needed to use the necessary room and was met in the hallway by a meowing feline. Little Miss Tiffany was telling her that it was time for tuna. So Mom went down to the kitchen and got the cat her treat. Mary heard Mom in the kitchen and asked, "Lou, what are you doing up at this hour?" My dear mother replied, "The cat wants her tuna!" Well, they had a big laugh over this and then both Grandmas went back to sleep. I couldn't wait to relate this to Brenda who laughed and commented, "Welcome to Tiffany's world!"

BOOK SIGNING TIME

Sunday morning, our 20th anniversary, was another nice, sunny day. I was up super early and Brenda got up pretty early, too. We got ready, packed up as much as we could, and went for breakfast at our favorite restaurant. We would be leaving for home soon after the book signing at the Expo, so we wanted to be prepared. The hotel staff had been excellent in accommodating us and told us that we could leave our car in the parking garage until 4:00 p.m. if we needed to.

We went back to the hotel after breakfast, loaded more stuff in the car, and walked down to the convention center. Being the last day, things were busy and the place was packed with wall-to-wall people. We went to Evergreen's station, greeted Brian, Keith, and Jeff and got set up for the day. I brought two 8 x 10 pictures of Taffy and Tiffany and we displayed them on a table where I was signing the books. My time was 10:30 a.m. to noon, but we ended up staying a half hour longer because people seemed interested in the book and hearing more about the cats. Cat lovers were intrigued with the book and many had questions about Taff and Tiff or had comments to make about their own felines. In all, I think I signed about 99 books and Brian and Jeff said this was good.

Some people were content with my autograph, but others asked me to write more on the inside cover, either to themselves, a relative or friend, or to their cat. To my surprise, Brian and Jeff were giving the books away, not selling them. Being a novice, I just assumed that they would be selling the books. Instead, it was a promotion to expose the public to my book and Evergreen Press. Starcrest of California had done much to publicize *Cats* and advertised it in one of their inspirational catalogs called *Traditions*. I was surprised at how many people in our area received *Traditions* catalog and saw the ad for the book. My mother's pastor, Viola Tyson, saw the advertisement and ordered the book. The ad was very well done and had an alluring appeal to cat lovers especially, and to anyone who cares about animals.

It was quite an experience to meet all kinds of people from all walks of life, many of whom were believers who rejoiced in a Christian cat book. Brian had told me that he knew of nothing like it on the market, that is, an animal book written from a Christian standpoint. The spiritual content of the book was what caught Brian's eye, and rightly so, because the message of the Gospel is of the most importance in any undertaking. The humorous stories about Taffy and Tiffany and other pets helped give the book a favorable attraction to the public in general. They made Brenda and I laugh and we thought other people, pet owners in particular, would enjoy them, too. As it turned out, we were right.

It was great also to work with Brian and Keith and Jeff. I am still amazed at how God brings believers together, and it is often in a business venture like this. What a difference and a pleasure it is to be involved with honest, upright, honorable individuals whose purposes and goals are on a higher level. It's a different world because Christians are not of this world, John 17:14. The philosophy is completely different from that of the world. Everything is above board with total honesty and integrity, and a sincere concern for the interests of others (Philippians 2:4). It isn't perfect, of course, but it is by far the best system in this troubled world.

So it was terrific to be with these fine gentlemen, believers redeemed by the precious Blood of Jesus Christ, dedicated to furthering His Kingdom by providing good, wholesome, and worthwhile reading material. Quite contrary to the sentiment I once heard a retail chain president offer that, "Nice guys finish last!" here are three "nice guys" who are successful and flourishing and blessed by God. I thank Him for bringing them into our lives. We are better people for it.

SO LONG NEW YORK CITY

We didn't want to leave! We had a wonderful time at the Expo and in New York. We would remember it for a long time, and we thanked the Lord again for the opportunity!

After saying good-bye to our three friends, we walked back to the hotel, got our car, and headed home. Brenda took some more nice pictures as we left the city, passed through the Lincoln Tunnel, and entered into New Jersey. She called home on our new cell phone and told my mother that we were on our way. Later, people asked me how I liked driving in New York City, and I said I didn't really know. I couldn't give an honest opinion because I had no real experience to draw from. I drove a total of three miles in New York—a mile and a half in, and a mile and a half out. Once we parked the car in the hotel garage, it never moved until we left. But don't get me started on taxi cab rides! There oughta' be a law....

However, we survived and are alive to tell the story. We won't forget the great time we had with Scott on Friday night, and as a token of our appreciation, we bought him a copy of Les Miserables—unabridged! We had told him about the book and the musical and how intriguing the story was with the setting at the time of the French Revolution. We wish him the best in all that he is doing with God's blessing. He is a fine young man and I am sure he will be successful.

Isn't life incredible? Isn't God incredible? Little did we know that we would be here at this point in time when Taffy and Tiffany came into our lives in April of 1987. The thought of writing a book about them never occurred to me until some years later. It was of course an answer to prayer inspired by Dr. Norman Vincent Peale. He wrote, "If you are experiencing financial difficulty, don't ask God to let you win a lottery or a sweepstakes; ask Him for insight and ideas." I asked the Lord for those two things and once, while reading a cat book, the idea came to me to write my own book about Taff and Tiff. Now, here is the second book about those two fantastic felines!

Dr. Peale's principle is smart, sound, sensible advice—and, it's Biblical. The thrust of the counsel is this: Don't look for a quick fix, the easy way out; look to God for wisdom to use your own abilities and gifts which He has given to you. Paul the Apostle tells us:

God will give you insight...Work with your own hands...(2 Timothy 2:7; 1 Thessalonians 4:11).

God doesn't hand us everything on a silver platter. He knows that it is better for us to pray and plan and work, and have the satisfaction that we have used our skills wisely to achieve something worthwhile. When we have done our best, worked hard, did what was right, and come up short of our needs, then God steps in and provides what is beyond our reach or control. Check out Philippians 4:19.

The Lord is faithful, reliable, trustworthy. He wants to bless us abundantly. He wants to open His storehouses in heaven and pour out more blessings that we can handle, Malachi 3:10. We need to obey, turn to His Son in faith, receive Him as Savior, follow His commands, live for Him, and ask Him to show us what life is really all about. Want a little advice? "Get ready!"

CHAPTER 8

TIFFANY TRIES TO FILL THE GAP

It was difficult for us to give up our beloved Taffy, and it is still painful when we think of her or notice some of her things. Like most people when a loved one or a pet dies, we do not want to accept it, and at first, even try to deny it. To say that we were attached to Tassers is to say the least. We certainly needed the comfort and support of the Lord and His people during our time of mourning—and we got it! But we did not think of someone else who might be mourning, too.

I guess we were too concerned about our own sorrow to notice Tiffany looking for her sister, or wonder just what she was going through. When we recovered from the initial shock that Taffy was gone, we began to watch Tiffy to see how she was handling the separation. We observed her going from one place to another, spots where Taffy slept or claimed as her own. She had the expression of a little lost soul. We were not sure how to help her or really what to do about her missing her buddy of nearly 15 years. We decided to confer with our good friend, Dr. Salzmann.

We felt a check-up was in order for Tiffany after a few weeks had passed since Taffy was put to sleep. An appointment was made to have the Tiffers checked out and to give us an opportunity to ask Dr. Salzmann some questions. He suggested giving her some extra attention and removing Taffy's toys from Tiffy's sight and smell. We had put most of the toys and items that Taffy liked in her casket, but we checked for more things that might make it difficult for our "Little One." We asked Dr. Salzmann about mentioning Taffy's name, and he thought it a good idea to try not to say it too much if we could help it. He said like humans, the mourning period for pets has to run its course. We know from reading about cats that they have good memories. They do not forget too easily. Tiffany would not soon forget Taffy.

It was very hard for Brenda and I to not mention Taffy's name. After being such a vital part of our lives for nearly 15 years, and talking to her many times a day, how could we refrain from saying her name, at least in Tiffany's hearing, that is. We knew that this was going to take some doing. But then we had to think of the kitty instead of ourselves. Again, cats are easily traumatized by actions or words, so we knew that we had to tread lightly. Easier said than done!

One evening, we were watching TV downstairs and I said something about Taffy. Tiffer was dozing on my lap and as soon as the word was out of my mouth, she was wide awake and staring at me with those big eyes. I looked over at Brenda and managed to utter, "Oops!" I felt very badly and Tiff did not make it any easier because she kept staring at me. I petted her and talked to her and finally she looked away and resumed her nap. However, a notable incident took place a month later when her reaction was the same. Yours truly experienced pangs of guilt again and tried to console the kitty. Many slip-ups have taken place since then, and we try to caution each other and make sure we know where Tiffy is before we talk about her sister. As pet owners know, it is hard.

At this point in time, little Miss Mowlskers seems to be doing better, but we still see her looking around and sitting and sort of staring into space. Of course we don't know how much she may search the place when we are not there. We can't read her mind either so we do not know what she is thinking. We just smother her with love and get her checked out if she acts strangely or appears not to feel good. We want to hold on to her as long as we can.

"KATARACT KITTY"

We had Tiffany in for a check-up at the animal hospital and Dr. Salzmann noticed that our little furball was developing cataracts. Brenda and I wanted to know when he thought they should be removed. He told us that animal medicine is not that far advanced yet and probably veterinarians would not attempt such surgery except in extreme cases. He explained to us that we should put drops in her eyes twice a day to counteract the dust particles in the air that Tiffany is not seeing now due to the cataracts. Normally, a keen-eyes cat will see the dust particles and close its eyes to avoid them.

Brenda, who is always checking Tiffy over as she did with Taffy, noticed more of a build-up or residue in the corners of her eyes. With the Kitty not seeing the dust in the air, she didn't close them or blink, and so the dust went right into her eyes. The natural moisture in her eyes washed the particles to the corners where it accumulated in nasty looking little lumps. Upon finding these tiny heaps of dust, Brenda cleaned them out with her finger or a cotton swab. Of course the kitty did not appreciate this procedure, and if Tiff suspected that Mommy was going to operate on her, she made herself scarce. She didn't care any more for the ear cleaning Mommy forced upon her from time to time. However, both necessary evils were needed to prevent more serious problems.

With Tiffany we haven't noticed any problems with her eyesight. She will catch something you throw to her or bat it back to you like she always did. When my boxer, Rinny, developed cataracts, his sight was impaired quite severely. If you stood in front of him and moved to one side or the other, he sat for a few seconds staring at where you were, and then he turned to where you moved. We have not seen Tiff doing anything like that. So we will continue the drops and clean her eyes and observe her to make note if the problem worsens.

TIMIDLY TRYING TO FILL THE VACANCY

It is interesting and satisfying to see the changes in Tiffany since she became the top-dog—or "cat"—in the Shaffer household. As I said before, she lived in Taffy's shadow for many years, and a lot of that was our fault. We catered to Miss Multi-colored and, perhaps without realizing it or meaning to do it, we neglected Tiffany. The Taffers just demanded your attention, and we usually gave in to her. Now, with Taffy gone, the little gray furball is getting all the consideration and is soaking it up like a sponge.

The sleeping arrangement is a good example of how things have changed. Taffy always slept at the head of the bed while Tiffany was at the foot. Now Brenda and I do not stay in one position all night long, and usually sometime during the evening or early morning hours, the cats would leave. After I began to sleep in my recliner downstairs, there was more room and the kitties started to spend the entire night with Mommy. The arrangement did not change, however, and Taffy retained her position right next to Brenda's head. The pussycats just had more room without Daddy taking up space in the bed, but Tiff remained at the foot.

When we invited Tiffers to the head of the bed—the space now vacated by Taffy's departure—she slowly and sheepishly walked up from the foot as if this was new, uncharted territory. With some coaxing and a lot of TLC, we persuaded her to lay down and feel confident about being there. At first, she still went to the foot at bedtime, and we encouraged her to come up to the head, and gradually she accepted the new arrangement. More recently, she even stays at the top if I feel good enough to sleep in the bed instead of my recliner. Sometimes my acid reflux is better and I try to get some shut-eye in a horizontal position. My wife complains—only to me—that, "My husband doesn't sleep with me anymore!" She is right; maybe only one or two nights a week. But I have a very understanding spouse and she rates my health over her own wishes.

You may recall from Cats I—assuming you read the book—that I tried to get Tiffany to talk. As growing kittens, Taffy was the more vocal of the two and we became a little concerned about our non-meowing kitty. With some concentrated conversation directed right at her, we were able to get her to open up. In fact, she talked so much that we told people that we created a "meow monster." As the sole feline in our home, she has become even more verbose. It is quite cute and Brenda's mother, Mary, cannot believe how much noise comes out of one little cat.

Apparently, she thinks she has to report in and out to Mommy when she leaves the bed and comes back after going to eat and drink or use the litter box. She quite loudly announces her departure and her arrival each time, almost as if she is asking permission to go and return. When Taffy was still with us, Tiffy most always grunted out a distorted meow as she jumped off the bed or some other sleeping or observation spot. But she always came back quietly, usually never making a peep as she jumped back up. Who really know why cats do things? Who really knows why people do things? Psychology has helped tremendously in studying and analyzing the human mind and offering solutions to troubled individuals. Pet psychologists have also put in a lot of time working with animals and their owners and have made great strides in helping both pets and persons to work through problems and to establish better relationships.

In Tiffany's case, Brenda and I believe that she is in effect asking permission each time she comes and goes, still in some way living in Taffy's shadow. She is a bit sheepish as she jumps up with us and will announce her presence as she enters a room downstairs. Although she is exuding more confidence in many ways, she still is a bit timid. We have tried to inspire her with lots of loving—kisses and petting, holding her, baby talk—and rewards for jumping, playing, and even going to the litter box! It seems to be working with good success. We just need to be patient and to keep giving her attention and accolades.

THE NAP!

One day, the little one decided that it was time for Mommy to lay down and take a nap with her. Often, as pet owners well know, cats choose the most inopportune times to demand attention. On this particular day, Brenda was trying to get some things done upstairs, and it involved going from one room to another. The usually unassuming and unaggressive pussycat became relentless in her quest to persuade Mommy to sack out with her for a while.

She pursued Brenda from one place to another, meowling profusely, and jumping up on the bed in our room and the one in the spare bedroom. My dear wife tried to ignore her at first, thinking that Tiff would give up and go lay down somewhere by herself.

119

Normally, she was not this persistent—not like Taffy who would never take "no" for an answer. Apparently she had been watching and learning from her sister and now put what she observed to the test. The tenacity, the cute requests in forms of meows, the little face and those big eyes, all worked to lay a big guilt trip on Mommy who acquiesced and took a snooze with the Tiffers. My good friend, Foster Furman, who wrote "Stick-to-it-tiveness Succeeds," would have been proud of Tiffany who stuck to her plan and succeeded in landing her target in the sack. Foster's book, a chronicle on the Furman family and their cannery business, is a delightful account of the struggles and the successes of a Christian family, who by faith and dedication made God their partner in a venture that has lasted for generations. Furman Foods, Inc., still operates on the belief that if they make the Lord their number one priority, they will be successful and blessed in their enterprise and in their family lives as well. This is right out of the Bible—a Scripture principle: "Commit to the Lord whatever you are doing, and your plans will succeed" (Proverbs 16:3).

Many other passages of Scripture encourage us to make the Lord a veritable part of every aspect of our lives. He desires to be involved in the minute details we wouldn't bother Him with. He is our Heavenly Father who loves us with a perfect and everlasting love. He wants us to involve Him in everything concerning our lives and to consult Him about every decision and venture. Not only are we obligated to Him for all that He has done for us, it is to our advantage to include our great God in all we do. Divine wisdom, guidance, insight, ideas, and strength are priceless, and we would be crazy not to include Him in everything. Of course, I am not implying that we "use" God to become successful or achieve what we want. He would never go along with that anyway. Our real motive should be and must be love (1 John 4:19). In any event, Tiffany was successful in getting Mommy to take a nap because of her persistence. We can learn a lesson from le cat!

THE LEAP

One day, Tiffy was perched on Brenda's lap downstairs and had been there for quite a while. After some time having a kitty on your

120

lap can become uncomfortable, especially if the kitty likes to stretch out on your lower legs. It can cause cramping, numbness—pain! Tiff usually starts out on Brenda's lap and works her way down to Mommy's lower legs as she changes positions. Sometimes her little head ends up almost between Brenda's feet. Then as the time goes on, my poor wife feels the need to move a bit, but does not want to disturb the pussycat. Oh how we cater to her!

On this particular day, Tiff had been napping with Mommy for some time and the kitty was starting to feel very heavy. The human needed some relief! So my partner in life said to her, "Tiffy, Daddy's coming down to sit with you and take a nap!" Quicker than a flash, the little gray mowl was up on her feet and with a single bound leaped over the snack tray between our recliners and on to my chair. Once upon my recliner, the furball curled up and waited for Daddy. My spouse of 20 years then called upstairs to me in my study, "Daddy! Your kitty is waiting for you!" I came down to find Miss Tiffany lying on my chair, all ready to sack out with her Daddy. She greeted me with a resounding meow which seemed to say, "What took you so long?" Brenda's mother, Mary, was impressed by this episode and said, "She jumped over to Clair's chair right after you told her he was coming down to nap with her." Her favorite daughter quipped, "Of course, Mother, we didn't raise no dumb cats." I had to agree.

THE WALK

A few days later, our fabulous feline displayed her keen understanding once again. Brenda and I were upstairs on this Sunday afternoon and decided to go for a walk before supper. Tiffers was going through her, "I wanta' sack out with somebody," routine and kept meowing at us, mostly from our bed in the bedroom. Brenda tried to assure the pumped-up pussy cat that we would honor her request when we returned. "When Daddy and I get back, Daddy will sit with you on his chair downstairs. Okay?" I said to her, "Thanks for volunteering me!" She came back with, "You're welcome!" We both kissed the kitty on the head and started out on our walk.

Our usual course is to walk up Route 890 and around a few blocks of Hamilton, a small suburb of Sunbury, and back again. It is a distance of approximately two miles and gives us a brisk workout. We stopped en route to exchange some hellos with folks we knew and met along the way, and upon arriving back home, we noticed our neighbor Bill Shipman on his back porch. Bill had been having a lot of pain and problems with rheumatoid arthritis, especially in his legs and feet. Being a farmer and having a machine shop business, he has no choice but to spend a lot of time on his feet. We decided to say hello and see how he was doing. Barb heard our conversation and came out to join in. We found that Bill was on some strong medication that was helping, but it would not entirely take away the pain nor remedy the condition. Many times we have to endure the unpleasant maladies that life often deals out to us. It is still difficult for me to see nice people suffer.

I guess that we were gone for well over an hour, and I had forgotten about Brenda's promise to Tiffany. While my wife tarried a bit with Bill and Barb, I went to check on Mary and see if she was sleeping or ready for some chow. As I peeked around the corner to investigate the situation, I found Mary snoozing away, but that was not what really caught my eye. Also asleep was a kitty cat and I'll bet you can't guess where she was napping. Yep! Right on my recliner, exactly where Mommy told her Daddy would sit down with her.

I quietly sneaked out to the back porch and saw Brenda coming across the lawn. I put my finger up to my lips to signal her to come silently into the house. Once in the back room, I whispered to her to look around the corner into the living room. She peeked in and turned back to me to ask, "I wonder how long she has been there?" I shook my head in wonderment.

We went in to greet Mary and Tiffany, and Mary asked if Tiff was still on the chair. She informed us that Tiffers was down here almost before we were out the door. Mary said, "She looked out in the back room, saw that you were gone, and came in here and jumped up on Clair's chair. I guess she's been there ever since." Brenda explained to her mother what she had said to the kitty upstairs before we went for our walk. Mary just shook her head. We all wondered just what this little cat didn't understand! She wowed us once again.

122

GROWING AND GLOWING

As I stated before, it was satisfying to see Tiffany change, to open up a bit, to come out of her shell. Brenda and I were very glad to see the kitty become even more vocal and outgoing, mainly because we felt that we were partly responsible for her timidity. Now, after 15 years, Tiff was venturing into new territory for her, so to speak, and doing things she didn't do before. It was gratifying for us and somewhat therapeutic due to our guilty feelings.

One big step for our little girl was at bedtime when we played puff or bat-the-ball with Taffy. Tiffy would usually watch or meekly attempt to worm her way into the game. And customarily, she was lured away with a string or some other toy. Taffy was the main attraction and received all the attention while Tiffany was relegated to second fiddle again and again! How foolish and uncaring we were to neglect her and dote on Taffy all those years.

But Tiffers is a very forgiving pussycat and one evening after clearing off the bed, she jumped up and laid down at the foot right where Taffy used to lay for the game. Brenda and I were surprised and elated at this development and quickly accommodated our gray stuffins'. The game with the Taffers had graduated from a powder puff to crazy balls that Brenda found in the pet section of a store. As I described before, these balls were furry with a squishy center. Taffy loved them and chose them over the puffs. A smack with a front paw sent them flying through the air at high speed. I spent a lot of time retrieving them because they flew much further than the puffs.

As we discovered, Tiffer also preferred the crazy balls, and could clobber them quite well with either front paw. We had some reservations about playing this game with Tiffany since we found that she had cataracts. Not to be concerned! The kitty had no problem seeing the ball and enjoyed the game immensely. Apparently the cataracts did not really impair her eyesight, because she zeroed in on the ball and did not miss hitting one if it was in her range. After batting the ball, she followed its course with eagle-eye precision. We were very happy to share this information with Dr. Salzmann, who told us to continue her eye drops twice a day. They seemed to be helping.

The game caught on and Tiff came to expect it every night before going to bed. We did not disappoint her and let her choose the length of the game. We found, however, that the kitty would often want to play the game in segments. One night as we were playing with Tiffy, she got down to eat and drink and we thought the kitty was finished with the game. I picked up the ball and put it away, and we started to get ready for a good forty winks. Without warning, the furball was back and with a stentorian meow, she announced to us that the game was still on. She plopped down in the usual spot ready for action, offering up a few short mowls to let us know she wasn't going to accept "No" for an answer.

We put off going to bed and continued to humor the puddycat until she tired of the activity. Still feeling a bit guilty, we felt that we owed Tiffy a whole lot of consideration. We don't mind making concessions for her and are encouraged by her increasing forwardness. In our minds, she deserves the attention.

Brenda and I are pleased with her progress as the sole recipient of our affection, but are glad that in many ways she is the same old Tiffany. Often she still asks permission before jumping up on our laps and announces her entrance into a room with a somewhat subdued meow. Even though she has no competition, she forgets herself and reverts back to her old ways. We don't expect her to change completely, nor do we want her to. We love her, however she chooses to be. At over a decade and a half, our pussycat is growing emotionally and mentally, being more assertive, and doing well physically. And, I have noticed a certain glow in that pretty little face.

GETTIN' AWAY WITH MURDER?

I mentioned making concessions a couple of paragraphs ago. We were willing to go the extra mile for Tissie Toes, and our little squirt has made the most of it. This diminutive gray and white fluffball has eaten up all the special privileges. You may remember how she shows up at breakfast, lunch, and supper expecting a bite or sample of what we are having. Recently, the tidbit has become more of a "portion" as the kitty asks for more than just a tiny amount. We don't want her to have too much "people food," so Mommy puts the brakes on when she thinks the puss-cat has had enough.

When we bring in one of her dishes for lunch or supper that is the signal to Snicker Snackers, as we sometimes call her, that she is going to get a special treat. Once in a while she begs for a hand out at breakfast, but her treat is a small amount of tuna, and lately some other varieties of cat food, plus a dab of oleo. This tradition has gone on for a few years now, and the kitty likes the plan. In fact, if we are negligent in the dispensing of her choice morsels, she becomes quite verbal in letting us know. Taffy was not remiss in telling Mommy and Daddy if they were taking too much time in administering her morning apportionment of tuna. Now, her sister was developing into a demanding little demagogue. We weren't sure if we like all the characteristics of this metamorphosis. Brenda often says, "She's becoming more like you-know-who!"

At mealtime, Miss Pussyfoots has gotten more bold in enjoining us for a share of what we are having. One day, when I was away, Brenda had a cup of milk and set it on the table between our recliners. She and Mary were watching TV in the early afternoon and did not notice Tiffany make her entrance. The kitty jumped up on my chair and spotted the cup. Before Brenda knew what was happening, Miss Futzie Dutz—and I don't know how we came up with that appellation—practically had her whole head in the cup, finishing the small bit of milk.

"Mother! Look at this cat!" my wife called to Mary, who turned just in time to see the "Dairy Desperado" before she pulled out her head.

My mother-in-law could not help but laugh at her grand-cat. "That's cute," Mary said, and then added, "She would be one upset pusscat if she got her head stuck!"

I heard the story from the ladies when I arrived home and said to Brenda, "Tiff wouldn't have done that before. She's getting braver."

Mary piped in, "And whose fault is that?"

My dear mate, who always has an answer retorted, "Yours!"

Her mother asked "How did you come up with that conclusion?"

Brenda came back, "Because you are always encouraging her and egging her on to beg or help herself." Mary shielded her eyes, knowing that she was caught red-handed.

Yet, we both knew that most of it was our fault because we had been almost hand-feeding the kitty, letting her lick our dishes or clean out our bowls on our laps. We were giving her food on our bed, in her bed, on my desk, and other places, really pampering the pussycat. No wonder she thinks she can get away with anything. Both our mothers agree: Tiff is a "spoiled brat!" But as Brenda is quick to assert, "She's a sweet little spoiled brat!" And we know that Mrs. Shaffer and Mrs. Barnett concur—being Tiffy's "Grammy" and "Grandma," respectively—they have been won over by the fur-ball.

LIKE SISTER...LIKE SISTER!

We made more accommodations for our little Sweetie as time went on. When Taff was diagnosed with bladder cancer, I put a chair beside my desk so that she could be near me in my study. Taffy always liked to be right on my desk, demanding my undivided attention. Now Tiffy was insisting on jumping up and plopping smack dab in the middle of my big desk calendar. To keep her happy, I moved in a chair, hoping that this would allow her to be with me, but also let me do some work. It wasn't exactly what she had in mind, but she slowly accepted the provision and curled up beside me.

About a month later, we were getting ready to have the parsonage re-carpeted and were moving furniture from room to room. In the study along the inside wall, I have seven two drawer file cabinets with three small bookshelves sitting on two long formica table tops. After we removed the bookshelves, Tiff began jumping up on the table tops and lying down to watch me work at my desk. This, of course, gave her a higher vantage point to observe me, and it wasn't too much of a distance to hop over to the desk. Brenda felt sorry for the kitty who was lying on that "hard" surface, so she put a pillow out of a padded dog bed on the table top. Tiffer liked this amenity and used the pillow on a regular basis. Soon, Mommy brought the bed and put the pillow in it and made the kitty even more comfortable,. She then told me, "When we bring the bookshelves back in, you know you can't take that away from her." I looked over at Tiffany who was basking in her new sack-out spot near her Daddy and knew that my wife was right. When the bookshelves were returned to the study, I elevated one of the shelves above her bed so that she would have more room and not bump her head. I even put two reams of copier paper under the front part of the bed to raise it to the level of the bottom shelf. To what extremes we go for the benefit of our fraternizing feline!

Miss Multi-colored used to watch me leave in the morning to go for my coffee and study time at Jay's, the local restaurant I spoke of earlier in the book. Then she would often "cut loose," as Brenda and Mary put it, at the top of the stairway or downstairs in the living room, kitchen, or backroom. Needless to say, this obstreperous meowing was quite annoying, not conducive to one's sleep. Brenda called this profuse crying "the call of the wild." I explained to my wife and mother-in-law that although Taffy was domesticated, she was still an animal and there was an element of the "wild" in her. This explanation did little to appease the ladies who covet their sleep. Secretly, I thought it was cute!

Now I don't know if Taffy left some instructions or suggestions with Tiffany before she departed this world. In any event, we have been surprised to find the little one mimicking her sister in many areas. As I stated before, we weren't sure if all of this was a good thing. But when I saw Tiffy watching me leave in the morning—from her room window or my study window—I was happy and I waved to her like I always did the Taffers. However, after mentioning this cute augmentation in her behavior to Brenda and Mary, I was informed that she had also adopted the howling as soon as I was out of sight. Oops! Conversation closed! Sometimes silence is golden.

I shared with everyone in Cats I how Taffy would sit and stare at you for extended periods of time. It made you wonder what she was thinking and it was a bit discomforting. Many times when we came upstairs we would be met by Miss Stare-You-Down, sitting in the doorway to her room, looking quite stoical, and making direct and continual eye contact with you. Animal experts tell us that if we stare at our pets or any other animal, they will look away first. Well, these folks never met Taffy! This cat did not look away. We were the ones who usually broke eye contact.

Enter, Tiffany! Our little Miss Meek-and-Mild has been spotted sitting and staring at us from various places in the house. We are not accustomed to this from the gray and white furball. It is another indication of how she has adjusted to her new role of being the lone kitty of our household. She seems to feel more comfortable and confident in asserting herself, whereas before she was hesitant and indecisive. Brenda and I are glad to see the transformation. We like the "new Tiffany."

Yet another habit she has assumed—peculiar to her sister—is that of coming into the bathroom with me in the morning while I take my shower. Taffy waited patiently—well maybe not so patiently—until I was out of the tub so that I would lay on the floor and let her lick, chew, nuzzle, and roll on the wet hair on my head. This was known as "Taffy-time," and Tiffy was excluded from this exclusive club. Brenda, being more alert than I to what was happening with the kitties, made this astute observation: "There has been too much 'Taffy time' lately. Tiffers is being left out!" So we tried to alleviate this inequality by creating some games and special times just for Tiffany. I must admit that on my part I did not always stick to the bargain like I should have. But my wife is a good overseer, and she incessantly reminded me of our agreement—and my duty! Still, I'm sure I did not do the little gray kitty justice.

Now Tiffy does not get into the hair scene like her sister did, but she loves to have her Daddy all to herself. Tiffany time consists of purring and nuzzling and drooling and looking bleary-eyed as if on drugs. She expects me to pet her and to talk to her until she decides that she has had enough attention. Often I cut the time a bit short if she wants a lot of attention. I don't feel guilty about this because now Tiffy gets a lot of attention throughout the day—from all of us. We all agree, our little lover-dover deserves it, and we enjoy showering our affection upon her.

FUN CITY KITTY!

While skimming through my *Webster's Seventh Collegiate* dictionary and looking at different words for cats, I came across a term that I had never heard of. The word was "Grimalkin," meaning an old female cat.

So the first time I called Tiffany a Grimalkin, Brenda surprisingly said, "Say, what? What did you call her?"

"A Grimalkin," I answered, "an elderly female cat. I found the word in the dictionary." "

How quaint," the love-of-my-life replied.

"I thought so," I retorted.

Well, at that point, Tiffany was not acting anything like a Grimalkin. No one would think that our little senior citizen pussycat was 15 plus. She was running and playing and jumping like a much younger cat. She was becoming more respondent to us as we talked to her and made suggestions or asked her to do something. The kitty seemed ready to join in with us whenever we initiated a game, wanted to take a nap, gave her food, or went downstairs. She was Johnny-on-the-Spot, eager to be doing things with us. The old cat was learning new tricks.

One precious episode that tickled all of us was when yours truly had to heed the call of nature while watching TV one evening. Tiff was lying on my lap and I informed my wife that I had to make a pit stop. Brenda said to the kitty, "Come on, Tiffers, Daddy has to use the litter box." With that she crossed over to Mommy's lap, all the while keeping an eye on me. "He'll be back," Brenda assured her. As I reached the top of the stairway I heard a familiar voice say, "Someone is following you!" I stepped into the bathroom and cracked the door a bit and watched.

Our little cutems came up the steps and walked into her room, looked into the litter box, and then came over to the bathroom and pushed the door open. I had by this time retreated away from the doorway and was watching her approach the entrance. Once inside, she meowed and gave me a look of, "Oh, is this the litter box Mommy was talking about?" I couldn't wait to tell Brenda and Mary what the kitty cat did. Mary was a bit more astonished than Brenda, but then my wife knows just how smart her furball is.

When we tell her to come downstairs with us, she doesn't wait for us to go down first like she used to. Now she makes a beeline down the steps ahead of us and is waiting in the living room when we get there. If Mary is in her chair and sees Tiffany come zooming in, she usually says to us, "Pusscat didn't wait for you! She came running in here like she owned the place." Well, in the kitty's mind, she does. Sometimes when we arrive a short time later, we find her perched on one of our chairs with perked ears and big bright eyes, meowing as if to say, "What took you guys so long?" We are all happy to see her being a more take-charge kitty.

Our mischievous pussycat still likes to skutch us, especially when we start to go downstairs. From some hiding place she darts out and runs behind us at a very fast speed, emitting some form of a garbled meow. This surprise tactic seems to give her immense pleasure and satisfaction. Born with a natural sad face, when Tiff pulls off this piece of subterfuge, we can see a clearly different expression on her tiny mug! She loves her two monster rattle toys and her knockwurst, which looks like a sausage wrapped in netting and tied at both ends. It is laced with catnip, which of course, entices the feline to no end. We love to see the fire in her eyes when she tears into the toy, encouraged often by Mommy and Daddy. Needless to say, Brenda and I were elated to see a fun-loving feline emerge from a heretofore quiet recluse. She has thrilled us at the Shaffer household and we thank our heavenly Father for this little tyke who has brought us so much love and enjoyment. Our prayer, albeit partly a selfish one, is that Tiffany will be with us for a long time to come. We, however, leave that with our all-knowing, wise and loving God.

GOOD JOB, TIFFERS!

We still find Tiffy Toes looking for her sister and oftentimes seeming to miss Taffy considerably. It is painful for us to see her sitting in a place staring at a familiar spot where she was used to seeing her sister. Sometimes she naps in Taffy's favorite areas. I guess pets are much like people when a loved one or a companion dies. They go to the places where their dear ones used to go and hold on to things that belonged to them.

After Taffy died, Brenda brought a pair of stuffed kitties upstairs and put them on the bed. These two plush cats look somewhat like Taff and Tiff and, of course, that's why I bought them for Brenda. This action was designed to be a therapeutic crutch for my wife and I because having to give up the Taffers was a devastating blow. The stuffed kitty represents something tangible for us to hold onto, and in a symbolic way, retain our memories of the TassCat. We humans are strange creatures and we do weird things. We all try to deal with pain in our own way.

One day, not long after Brenda began putting the stuffed cats on the bed, we noticed Tiffany sleeping with the one that looks like Taffy. She cuddled up with it just like the two of them used to do when they sacked out together. Once, when I was in my study and Brenda was lying down with Tiffy, she called me to peek around the corner. Little Miss Nooker Do's was nuzzling and licking and grooming the Taffy look-alike. She put a lot of effort into caring for this stuffed stand-in. Tiff has not bothered with the cat that resembles her, although it is always on the bed with the other one. Now I am certain that she can tell the difference between a real cat and a plush one. Perhaps like us, our kitty is compensating, trying to anesthetize the gnawing pain of missing her sister.

Animals never cease to astound us with the God-given instinctive things they do, notwithstanding the unique heroic and loving feats they perform. Why I could write a book...hey...I did write a book about the exploits of our two pussycats! They have amazed and dazed us just with their actions here in the parsonage. One evening when we were visiting with Clara Boone and her son, Peter, she told us of a story about a mother cat that adopted a litter of newborn puppies. Apparently the mother wanted nothing to do with them and abandoned the helpless little tykes. The cat's own kittens had died and so she adopted the pups, nursed them, and carried them around. The TV reporter who narrated the account was quite taken with the mother cat's actions in rescuing the tiny canines. It is another instance in which animals leave us an example of compassion and caring and sacrifice. Many times they are more like the Lord Jesus than we are!

The Tiffers is doing a great job of filling the gap—the empty space in our hearts left by Taffy's absence. No, she cannot take the Taffer's place and Taffy could not take hers. Each cat has its own unique personality and characteristics. Our two were as different as day and night, and we loved them for it. We thank the Lord for giving us these little kitties who taught us so much and brought immense joy to our lives. They loved us and we have loved them and are better people because of their presence in the parsonage of a country preacher and his wife. I am convinced that our all-wise and loving heavenly Father designed it that way. We find this, of course, in the world of humanity—in a deeper and more meaningful manner.

No person can take the place of another individual—not really! This is especially true of Christians who are endowed with talents and abilities like everyone else, but also have been given supernatural spiritual gifts, 1 Corinthians 12:4-6. The spiritual gifts are what distinguishes the Christian from the non-Christian. These divine abilities, given and employed by the Holy Spirit, are for the benefit of each separate congregation. Our spiritual gifts are given to profit other Christians (1 Corinthians 12:7,11) not ourselves. Of course, people outside the Christian community, i.e., unbelievers, will benefit as well when Christians exercise their spiritual gifts through the Holy Spirit's power and guidance (1 Corinthians 14:23-25). Spiritual gifts are listed in Romans 12:6-8; 1 Corinthians 12:8-10;28-30;13:8;14:1-40; Ephesians 4:11; and 1 Peter 4:10-11.

It's wonderful how God has delicately designed and enabled us to live effectively in this world. Every person is unique and really irreplaceable. How unfortunate it is that so very many never discover this life-changing and life-enhancing truth. So many never come to a saving knowledge of the Lord Jesus Christ. This is a needless and foolish tragedy! The Savior is available to all who will come to Him (John 6:37). To God, every person is important—one of a kind. No other person can fulfill their purpose for being here on earth. If we do not realize that purpose and never complete it, someone else will come along in God's plan and program for mankind, but they will not do the job He intended. Only we can fulfill the purpose for which God placed us here. We are irreplaceable!

"Because God chose you..." (2 Thessalonians 2:13).

CHAPTER 9

IF YOU BELIEVE...

I t doesn't seem possible! How time passes! In April of 1987 we brought our two little squirts into the parsonage and began a wonderful relationship with a pair of furry speedsters. What a chore it was to keep track of energy-packed kittens! And fun! As I write this chapter it's hard to believe that was more than 16 years ago. Brenda and I framed a lot of memories with Taffy and Tiffany over the years and will treasure them the rest of our lives. And, as I said previously, when this whole thing is over and God brings His plan to fruition, I believe we will have all eternity to spend with them. A good friend of many years and a Bible scholar of scholars, Dr. Paul Kaiser, often said, "We have a glorious future!" Now that I have a few decades behind me and that future is closer, I can say a hearty amen!

LOOKING BACK

Who would have thought that two little kittens could have such an impact on our lives? I must add, too, a positive impact! But that is what happens when the Lord is working in your life. Oh how I wish that I would have allowed Him to work much more in my life and not hindered His purpose and blessings so many times. I wonder how much I have missed! Like many believers, I have cheated God—and other people as well by my unbelief, doubts, rebellion—sin! However, if I wallow in self-pity that is sin too. I must forget, learn from my mistakes, and go forward (Philippians 3:13). The Christian is to steadily progress in an upward direction, becoming more like the Lord Jesus (Romans 8:29). There is no higher goal.

Now, two books have been written about Taffy and Tiffany— "The Parsonage Cats"—and I am still a bit overawed by the whole thing, but rejoicing in what has happened over the past several years. I pray and hope that I have in some small way influenced others to step out in faith, work hard, and go for their dreams. May God bless you, reader, as you seek to realize your goals and visions of better and bigger things.

As I look back over the years, I chuckle as I recall an incident back in August of 1990. Brenda and I had spent the weekend with my parents who were celebrating their 50th wedding anniversary. My sister, Nancy, and I planned a Sunday afternoon drop-in at the church in Mom and Dad's hometown, and it was very well attended. This beloved and very popular couple would make it to 58 years before Dad passed away. I had been hoping that they would reach sixty. I thank the Lord for such good parents.

That evening we left to return home and ran into a bottle-neck on Route 80. For some reason the traffic was becoming funneled into one lane and was at a standstill. Taff and Tiff were in their pet taxi in the backseat and were crying, no doubt because the car had stopped, and they thought it was time to get out. We decided that it was okay, so Brenda opened the door and set the kitties loose. The little nuts came out in a flash and were up in the back window looking at the people in the cars around us. They ran all over the car, stretching their little necks to see what was going on, and practically falling over each other in the process.

The folks in the other cars caught sight of this two-ring circus and were laughing at our frolicking felines, enjoying the show. There were some children in a couple of the cars and they were totally taken with T and T. Brenda and I could not believe this surprising turn of events. Were these our shy kitties who hid when strangers were near? Now, they were only a few feet away from other humans and were acting like they were the main attraction in a sideshow. Our otherwise coordinated cats were so excited that they slipped and fell off the car seats, bumped into each other, and meowed up a storm. My vinyl seats did not help the situation. The pussycats could not maintain a secure footing. This was, of course, much to the delight of the spectators, who, like us, were in hysterics. We were almost sorry when the traffic started moving, and I think some of the motorists watching Taffy and Tiffany were a little sad to have to see them go. A few of them, especially the kids, waved to the frisky furballs as we all pulled away. We decided to let them have the run of the back of the car for the rest of the trip—something we didn't usually do because of safety reasons. This turned out to be a humorous mistake.

About an hour later, we pulled into the driveway at the parsonage and I went to open the door while Brenda attempted to put the kitties into their pet taxi. "Attempted" is the key word here. The car had stopped and this was like a flashing signal to the electrified fluff puffs. After unlocking the door, I came back to the car to witness this sidesplitting debacle. The tears rolled down my face as I watched my wife vainly try to corral these cavorting cats. At first, it was amusing to her too! She would manage to get one in the taxi, close the door without latching it, and try to catch the other one. The procedure did not work. The one in the carrier would either push the door open and escape, or get out when she went to put the other one in. It was another two-ring circus.

After some time, I saw my usually calm and collected spouse showing a bit of frustration. I was still laughing and enjoying her dilemma when she caught me in my revelry. The eye contact wasn't pretty. I knew the situation could turn ugly! I made haste to the car to assist her with these super-charged furballs. I know just how far I can push her, and I had let it go far enough!

I opened the car door carefully and got inside while Taff and Tiff were preoccupied with watching a bird or something in the yard. After I was in the car, we grabbed their little carcasses and stuffed them in the pet taxi—gently, of course. Their Sunday free-for-all was over and soon they were back in the confines of the parsonage. Once in the house, they settled down and decided to take a nap. We were very happy to see them a tad tuckered out and elected to join them.

Another cute episode took place when the two were kittens, only a few months old. Brenda was not home at the time and I was playing with them in the back room. I remember how big the room looked at that time. That is because it was quite empty—before we inherited so much from our parents and Brenda's Aunt Marguerite. Now, the back room is filled with furniture and "things" and looks much smaller. Then it made a great playroom for the kitties with lots of space to run and chase each other.

On this particular day I had confined Taff and Tiff to the room by closing the door that leads to the kitchen. We had made it into a Dutch door which was still too high for them to jump over. With food, water, toys, and a litter box, it made a good place to keep track of them. There was nothing in the room that presented any danger to curious, inquisitive kittens. At this point in time, they had their front claws but could not hurt the indoor/outdoor carpet one of our members had laid for us in this room. Since it was our main entrance into the house, we wanted something that would stand up to the traffic.

Yours truly was entertaining the tiny balls of fluff—and being entertained—with various cat toys, watching them go after the balls and catnip mice, etc. Although they were quite young, I was trying to train them to chase and fetch, without much success. At this stage of the game, they were reluctant to give up any of the toys. Every once in a while they would get into a "wrasslin' match," much to my delight, and some rough ones at that. Even though they were just kittens, they got a bit serious about these sporadic tussles. If they ruffled each other's fur, it was soon forgotten and they were back playing as usual.

At one point, I intercepted Taffy when she came close to me and started to wrestle with her. The little tyke ate this up and kept me on my toes trying to avoid her sharp claws and teeth. From time to time, she would growl and let out a distinct meow as if she was quite provoked. I was not hurting her in any way, but apparently someone thought I was. Without any warning, I felt an acute pain in my right heel—being in my stocking feet—the victim of an attack from the rear. Tiny Miss Tiffany came to her sister's rescue by biting me in the heel, and I must say the affront was quite effective. She got my attention! I responded with an "Ouch!" and released Taffy who scampered away.

When Mommy came home, I could not wait to tell her about the dastardly little demon—her child—who pusillanimously assaulted me from behind. If I was hoping to receive any pity from my better half, those hopes were dashed to pieces in prompt fashion. She picked up the furball and held her face to face and said, "Good goin', Tissy!" What compassion! What support! What ah' bummer! We had a lot of good laughs over the episode, and still do, and share it quite often with other cat lovers.

Yet another amusing incident which I did not relate in Cats I, took place after the kitties' first trip south to Lancaster. I call it amusing now, although it was not funny when it happened. This also took place in 1987 during their "kittenhood," and we won't soon forget it.

We had returned from visiting Brenda's parents and after unpacking and settling in for the evening, we were watching Taff and Tiff play with their little house in the living room. I was sitting on the sofa and Brenda was across from me on one of the over-stuffed chairs. We were congratulating our two little kittens on how well they did at Grammy and Grandpa's as they zoomed in and out of the house, batting at each other and running up and down the ramp inside. They were having a ball.

Then, all of a sudden, the complexion of the situation changed. One of the two critters must have done something awry. Whatever happened, we now had a pair of irritated kitty cats—no!—they were enraged! Talk about a pace off! Brenda and I were aghast! I had never seen kittens so angry before in all my born days. These two meant business! We sat for a long minute in stunned silence, not really believing what we were seeing. And what we were seeing was arched backs, fur standing up on end, flattened ears, wide eyes filled with fury, and buffed tails; not to mention what we were hearing—blood-curdling growls, mean meows, and hissing.

From experience, I knew what two cats—small or large—could do to each other. I did not want that to happen here to Taffy and Tiffany. After regaining my composure, I began to talk to them, trying to divert their attention from their anger and hoping to get them to forget whatever sparked the confrontation. Brenda reached out for one of them, but I quickly cautioned her not to touch either one because they would transfer their hostility to her. A cat usually strikes out at whoever is nearest to them when they are angry or frightened. At this point, our best strategy was sweet talk and hope for the best.

Just as I was about to go to the back room to get a pair of work gloves in case the fur started to fly, the conflict was over. (Protective covering is very helpful in such situations involving cats. If your feline has front claws, especially, be aware that they are razor sharp and can do much damage. Gloves and heavy clothing can prevent unnecessary scars and scratches when disarming a fight, giving medicine, or performing some other activity with a kitty.) Brenda and I both ushered up a sigh of relief, glad that our little girls were back to normal.

We have related this story over and over to people, cat lovers and folks who do not have cats or know anything about them, and it always cracks them up. Yes, we can laugh now because the incident is in the past. They never got into it like that again until the "Big Cat Spat" in *Cats I*, Chapter Nine—and we have often said to ourselves perhaps this early squabble was a prelude to that "cold war" which lasted a year and a half. On the bright side of that unpleasant period, we learned some valuable lessons about raising cats and about life in general. Truly, we are never too old to learn. We have many more fond memories of Taff and Tiff, cute stories that we will always cherish—too many to share here.

When I told people that I was writing a sequel to the Cat book and the new adventures of "The Parsonage Cats," someone remarked, "How much can you write about two cats who live in a house and who never get outside? After a while you'd have to make some of it up!"

I quickly replied, "Not with Taff and Tiff! With those two there is never a dull moment. They just keep giving us more memories and more material. I'll never have any problem writing about them!" And that is the truth, they have been just remarkable!

CATS AND THE CHRISTIAN FAITH

Brenda and I had been married about ten months when the district manager of our drug company offered me a job as assistant general manager of a store in Lancaster County. I accepted the job, after conferring with my newly-wed wife, attracted by the huge salary that went with it. A week later, the vice president of human resources came to see me about another position as personnel manager in the main office in Northumberland County, about 100 miles away. After treating my spouse to a second steak dinner in a local eatery to discuss the new development, we decided on the second offer. Within weeks the company moved us into Selinsgrove, a town right across the Susquehanna River from Sunbury and Northumberland.

This all took place in early 1983 and for the first year in our new surroundings, we tried to become acclimated to our new jobs, the different area, and the big change in our lives. The Tri-County region of Northumberland, Snyder and Union was not the embodiment of a Lancaster County where everything was available and at your fingertips. I was concerned about Brenda's adjustment as a "City Girl" to small town America. No problem! She adapted and made herself at home. I had been raised in a rural area not too far away and was used to country life. We settled in and looked to God and what He had for us at this juncture of our lives.

As a Christian, I am keenly aware of the providence of God in the affairs of men, especially His redeemed children. I like to think of it as His "Divine Superintendence." The Bible says that,

A man's heart plans his course of action, but the Lord directs his steps (Proverbs 16:9).

Brenda and I had been praying for some kind of ministry since I finally finished up my schooling for my bachelor's degree. Within a year and a half I had acquired my master's degree and was looking to the Lord for a way to serve Him in more than just an occasional preaching job. I felt that I had failed Him big time, and I was hoping that He would give me another chance to use the gifts and abilities He had given me. Our heavenly Father doesn't like to see any of His children sitting on the shelf, being of no use. That is not good for Him, for them, or His people and Kingdom.

Like the loving and forgiving God that He is, the Lord opened up a two-church pastorate in early 1984 through an old friend, Barry Mutschler, who, ironically, also worked for the same drug company Brenda and I did. Barry was a member of our St. Elias Church and knew of my background in the ministry. He introduced me to some of the church leaders and the rest is history. God's providence in our lives came more clearly into view when the drug company was sold and a lot of us lost our jobs. The promotion, the move, the sale of the company—it all made sense. He hadn't brought us here to work in retailing—that was just a vehicle leading to the ministry we were praying for. And that ministry involved all of the wonderful folks we have been privileged to serve at Zion and St. Elias.

Of course, then in April of 1987, the Lord plopped two little kittens in our laps who would affect our lives in an astounding way. Many times it is the small things in life that God uses to reach us and make us aware of His plan and purpose in this world. I am sure that most animal experts and pet lovers would agree that the greatest lesson our furry friends teach us is unconditional love. Perhaps among the many reasons for which God put them here, the most important one stands out as unconditional love. Isn't this the paramount need of the earth? Isn't this why God sent His Son, to show us that love through the power of the Savior is the answer to the manifold maladies of mankind? Certainly!

God has not left Himself without a witness. The most notable testimony to His existence and surpassing love is human beings who are created in His image. We homo sapiens have the capacity, with His help, to change the world, to make a difference—to represent God and to declare His glory. The universe and our own planet testify to God's love and majesty. He has given us so many evidences of His work and presence.

And if we are paying attention, our cats, dogs, gerbils, parrots, pigs, turtles, horses, iguanas, and so many more, will demonstrate to us that God is here and that He means us no harm. We would do well to heed their instruction and follow their example. The ordinary person who has never had a pet, or never thought of his pet as being more than just an animal, will miss seeing the providence of God in bringing an adorable critter into his life. Many people never realize the purpose of their own existence let alone the design of the Creator for everything present in His wonderful world. Now that's worse than a misfortune—that's a travesty.

Brenda and I are so happy that we became aware of God's providence in bringing Taffy and Tiffany into our lives. Besides the love and all the fun and entertainment and adventures they have given to us, the many stories and sermon illustrations—and, of course, the two books—we cannot describe the exhilaration these two little rascals brought to us over the years. They certainly have been the source of many of God's blessings to us and we thank Him for them.

And, I see His hand in directing our path in meeting Thelma Deroba, a member of our Zion Church. This wonderful Christian lady is an excellent example of what a human being should be. She is so much like the Lord Jesus in every area of her life that it is a blessing to be around her. "Father, send us more Thelmas!" After we took Taff and Tiff into the parsonage and Thelma realized how much we loved cats, she loaned us cat books on a regular basis. We learned a lot about our feline friends in reading these books, and it was through one of them that I was inspired by the Lord to write Cats I. Brenda and I thank Thelma for her thoughtfulness in sharing her many books with us.

It was through the encouragement of Dr. Norman Vincent Peale and Dr. Robert H. Schuller that I dared to undertake the task of writing a book in the first place. I wrote to Mrs. Ruth Peale to express my appreciation for Dr. Peale's positive influence. I also wrote to Dr. Schuller, thanking him for his motivating books and messages. Thanks be to God for Christian men like these fine gentlemen who dedicated their lives to the service of the Lord and to helping people. Their rewards in heaven will be great!

When I was looking for a publisher, and preferably a Christian company, my friend June Maneval, owner of the Bible Depot store in our city, suggested Destiny Image in not too far away Shippensburg. The very nice folks at Destiny Image took the time to write a two page letter explaining that they do not publish books such as mine, but recommended Genesis Communications. I am grateful to them for the lead which has resulted in two books and a friendship with fine Christian people. It has been a pleasure to work with Brian, Kathy, Jeff and Keith, and see not only my dream come to fruition, but also to be part of an effort to provide a biblical witness to the public through the printed page. I pray every day that the books will reach many people for the Lord Jesus Christ.

It is thrilling to see the providence of God in planning and providing everything we need as believers to reach out and achieve great things for Him. It is satisfying to be one of His servants and to experience His power, wisdom, and guidance. How can we ever thank God enough for everything He has done for us? Of course, the answer is we cannot, but let's try!

The Lord Jesus said, "If you believe, you will receive!" (Matthew 21:22) This is the key to unlocking the fathomless treasures of God. He can bless and reward the feeblest of faith, so do not hesitate, do not wait, go to Him and make your requests, your hopes, your dreams, your heart's desire a prayer to Him. He is waiting to bless you beyond anything you can imagine.

When you are a member of the Christian faith, that is, God's family, you have been ushered into a different realm. You are still in this world, but you are no longer of this world. See John 15:19 and 17:14. You have been liberated and elevated to a higher level of existence. God's power and blessings are at your disposal. Your part is to believe and obey. Then things begin to happen! We might say that "God" begins to happen in your life! Sometimes it is big and sometimes it is small. Always it is a blessing and above the ordinary.

After I wrote *Cats in the Parsonage*, people I didn't really know came up to me and shared their "cat experiences" with me, telling me how much they enjoyed the book. My circle of friends was enlarging, and I thanked the Lord for the new and interesting folks He was sending my way. Many of these were Christians and I thought how wonderful it was how God could use two kitties to bring believers together.

One day when I was at one of my favorite restaurants, the manager gave me a note from a little girl named Olivia. She had left it for me, having missed seeing me on one of the days I am usually there. The note was to let me know that she was so happy that I loved animals and especially cats. Her note, complete with some hand-drawn pictures, read like this:

> To: Rev. Shaffer
> Thank you.
> I know how you feel about animals.
> I have one cat (Delilah) and two dogs (Zen & Jack).
> From: Olivia Lynne Best

I wrote back to Olivia, thanking her for her note and for sharing her pets with me. I told her that I hoped to meet her some day and talk about our furry friends. My wish came true not long afterward when Olivia came into the restaurant with her Grandmother, Christine Blank, a friend of ours, and wife of Jerre Blank, our local mortician. I am always impressed with young people and how more advanced they are these days. Olivia is a pretty, bright, and informed young lady who is a pleasure to talk with.

Another time in a phone conversation with Brenda's brother, Bill, I learned that his daughter, Ashley, had written a book report on *Cats in the Parsonage*. Bill and his wife, Beverly, live in York, PA, with their twin daughters, Ashley and Erin. Bill is a bank trust officer and Beverly is a medical technician. Personally, I had never thought of "Cats" as being book report material, but again, this is an example of the ingenuity and creativity of our young people today. They never cease to amaze me. I was flattered by Ashley's insight and efforts, and thanked the Lord that the book was put to another good use. Bill and his family are cat lovers too.

Brenda's oldest brother, Jim, and wife, Madge, live in Atkins, Virginia, and are animal lovers as well. Jim is a blacksmith and tinsmith with his own shop, and has gained wide recognition for his work. Madge, educated in industrial relations, has been employed by such corporations as Caterpillar and IBM. Due to some health problems, she has had to take her retirement prematurely. Jim and Madge also have two daughters, Emily and Catharine, who are married and doing quite well for themselves. Both Jim and Bill, and their families, have been to visit with us at the parsonage, happy to see that Mary is content and in good health.

While visiting with Florence Reitz, a member of our Zion Church, who lives with her daughter and son-in-law, Judy and Paul Elsasser, I was pleased to see that they had a dog and cat. Lady, the canine part of the family, is a little terrier who just loves company and attention. Lady always greets you and makes you feel right at home. The kitty, Peppie, checked me out when I made my first couple of visits, and like many felines, perhaps thought, "Oh, it's him again! He's old hat!" My own cats have done that to me, and I learned not to be offended because it is often just the "cat's way." After sharing and comparing stories and characteristics of our pussycats, I showed them some pictures of Taffy and Tiffany that I carry with me. People always like to see what our two furballs look like, and I am ready and more than willing to accommodate.

On one visit, Judy asked me if she could keep a photo of each of the cats to paint a picture on wood for us. I was very happy to loan her a couple of the photos, eager to see what Judy had in mind. Once, when Brenda accompanied me to visit Florence, Judy showed us some slate paintings she had done for one of her church's ladies groups. We were quite impressed! And when she completed the wood cut out of the cats, with Taffy on one side and Tiffany on the other, we were doubly impressed and very appreciative. Judy captured their features skillfully, and we will treasure this gift for the rest of our lives.

I told Judy and Paul that the talent runs in the family, and on my next visit, I took the wooden wall hanger Florence painted and the framed calligraphy of John 3:16, artfully done by her younger daughter, Peggy. These gifts were for Christmas one year and are displayed in the parsonage. We have formed a great friendship with Florence, Judy, and Paul, and are ever grateful and amazed at how God brings us together in love and fellowship. Cats and the Christian faith? Boy, that sounds good! Cats and Christians just seem to go together. Of course, I could be a tad bit prejudiced.

"IF YOU BELIEVE..."

It sounds so simple, doesn't it? And it is! But then for some, it isn't. They have trouble believing because they have spent so much time unbelieving! It is very difficult for these people to exercise faith, to think positively, or to accept the unconditional promises of God. It is a tough mindset to break away from, but with God, all things are possible. I always direct such individuals to Matthew 17:20.

And He said to them, "Because of your unbelief? For truly I am saying to you, if you have faith like the grain of a mustard seed, you will say to this mountain, 'Move from here to there,' and it will move! And nothing will be impossible for you!"

Lack of belief or lack of faith cripples a person's attitude on life and his ability to achieve the goal God has set for him. However, the Lord Jesus tells us that He will accept faith the size of a mustard seed. What a deal! A person would be foolish not to take it. What happens then, after trying it God's way? The impossible becomes possible.

One of our St. Elias families was on vacation, traveling through Georgia. They were on an interstate four lane highway, which was a popular route and at this time was quite busy. The mother was driving with her daughter in the front and dad in the back seat. All of a sudden, a car driven by a woman—no other people were visible in the vehicle—pulled alongside of them and the driver motioned for them to pull over. You can imagine their reaction to this situation. They were in another state more than 1000 miles from home, and a person they never saw before was asking them to pull over to the side of the road. Reluctantly, but for some reason they felt that they should comply with the woman's request. After pulling to the side, the woman pulled in front of them, got out, and ran up to their car. She motioned for the mother to roll down the window, which, with some hesitation, she did.

The stranger then proceeded to deliver a startling speech to an already startled family. "I can see that you are struggling with something, but I want you to know that it is going to be okay. Do not be afraid, everything is going to be all right." She looked at the man in the back and said, "You are a wonderful father. You are both good parents!" Looking at all of them, she encouraged them, "Don't worry, things will work out fine! You're going to have a wonderful time on your vacation."

She then shocked them even further with this pronouncement: "Many of the people driving by on this highway are not going to the same place we are. They are not going to the wonderful destination we are. So do not be afraid—there are some great things ahead in store for you."

With that, she returned to her car and waited for them to pull out on to the interstate. They sat there for a moment in stunned silence and then pulled out onto the highway. They all looked back to watch the stranger pull out behind them—perhaps partly to make sure she made it safely, and maybe also due to an irresistible curiosity. With an eerie lull in traffic on this busy freeway, they checked again on this enigmatic lady who seemed to know so much about them.

It had only been a moment—no time at all—but suddenly there were no cars behind them. The woman was gone! Disappeared! Vanished! Nowhere to be found! An uneasy chill came over them as they realized that they had not passed any exit ramps or emergency turnoffs. There was no place she could have gone—but she was gone! It was very quiet for a while as they sped along I-95, each one pondering just what had happened.

Who was that woman? Or perhaps more accurately, what was that woman? An angel? A messenger from God? A concerned Christian? Who was she? Where did she come from? Why did she single them out from all the vehicles on the interstate? How did she know so much about them? What were these "great things" that were in store for them? What did all this mean? What was the purpose of this uncanny encounter? These questions and more would haunt them for some time to come.

When they related the story to me, I thought immediately of another such incident I had heard about over 30 years ago involving two Christian men. I won't share that story here, but the circumstances were similar. I believe that our friends had a meeting with an angelic visitor. Why? Only God knows for sure, but perhaps it was to encourage them and strengthen their faith. When our heavenly Father goes to all this effort on behalf of His children, it has to be important, and the effects are always far reaching.

Later on, they found out that the mother was expecting, and with the daughter being around ten years old, an ecstatic excitement came over them. Was this one of the great things the woman spoke of? Did God have some other great surprises in store for this family? Only time would tell! And remember the Lord Jesus' promise in John 1:50, "Greater things than these you are going to see!"

The occurrence has had a profound effect upon our blessed trio, and upon many of us at St. Elias. God knows that we need a shot in the arm once in a while to boost our faith and to shake us out of our spiritual passivity. So every so often He throws a miracle at us. Our part then, is to thank Him and act on His goodness and purpose.

This popular and well-liked family continue to enjoy the results of their mysterious rendezvous and are the better for it. They know they were the recipients of God's special favor, and they are grateful! Ironically, they are also animals lovers and have several pets, and a couple of these came into their lives in a less than ordinary way. It all comes together and then some…"If you believe!"

CHAPTER 10

IN CONCLUSION

"In conclusion!" It sounds so final. In some ways it seems to echo a note of discord—the end to something good. And in America we do not like endings. We hate to see the end of a good movie, the end of a great play or musical or concert, the end of a super football game in which our team sparkled, or the end of the Fourth of July celebration where Lee Greenwood sang "God Bless the USA!" For Christians, we hate to see the end of an inspiring church service or the conclusion of an evangelical crusade. We Americans, for the most part, are used to the "good life," to having the benefits of freedom and all the perks that go with it. We forget that for many people around the world, life is just one bad day after another—a hellish nightmare they wish would end! For them, "In conclusion," is almost a blessing. We have to admit that our pets have it better—much better—than millions of people on this troubled planet. We need to pray and support efforts to alleviate their oppression and suffering. This is part of the Christian's mission. See Ephesians 4:28, "Farewell...for now."

In conclusion! Even for Christians there is a conclusion, a final curtain, if you will, to this life. Like other people, Christians do not like to give up their loved ones or close friends, but they know there is a limit to this earthly life. Solomon, the preacher-king of Israel, said it quite eloquently.

In Conclusion

There is a time for all things, and a season for every action under heaven. A time to be born and a time to die (Ecclesiastes 3:1-2).

Last year, Darlene Reffeor was called home to be with the Lord, and later, Donna Kistler, entered into the presence of the Savior. Both battled that dreaded disease of cancer and fought it nobly and with dignity. They both were employees of the Sunbury Animal Hospital and are sorely missed by family and friends alike. These two elegant women were of great assistance to Brenda and I, and Taffy and Tiffany, too. They cared and people knew it. We loved them dearly in the Lord.

Believers feel pain and sorrow and go through a period of mourning like everyone else but realize, however, that physical death is not the end of human existence. There is more after this life, and God's children receive comfort and confidence from the words of the Lord Jesus Christ,

Because I Myself am living, you also will continue to go on living (John 14:19)

Knowing that we have all eternity to look forward to puts a different slant on facing death or accepting the passing of someone we love and cherish. We experience the assuring challenge of Paul the Apostle:

Where, O death, is your triumph? Where, O death, is your sting? (1 Corinthians 15:55).

So to Darlene and Donna, we say, "Farewell for now." We repeat the consolation of Peter Marshall to wife, Catherine, on the eve of his death, "I'll see you in the morning!" We rest upon the promise of God that we will be reunited in heaven forever.

"Memories Are Made of This," is the title to a popular song of some years ago. For Brenda and I, many memories are made of the wonderful times we have had with our beloved friends, Taffy and

149

Tiffany. One of my favorite scriptures, Job 12:7 says, "Ask the animals and they will teach you." We certainly have learned much from them.

May God bless you as you make lots of great memories with your pet.

About the Author

Clair Shaffer was born and raised in rural, central Pennsylvania. While working his way through college, he raised a cat and began to appreciate all her quirks and delights. He had a wide variety of work experiences and enjoyed being a manager of personnel for a retail store where he worked with his wife Brenda for three years before they were married. Almost 20 years ago, he took a temporary position as a pastor of two churches and has been with them ever since.

Clair has loved writing all his life, having kept a sports notebook containing game details and stats of the local team from the last 45 years. After reading numerous cat books, he decided that his cats, Taffy and Tiffany, lived as exciting a life as any he had read about and began to put their lively escapades down on paper. This book is a continuation of the original *Cats in the Parsonage.*